Hire the Right Faculty Member Every Time

D1214441

Hire the Right Faculty Member Every Time

Best Practices in Recruiting, Selecting, and Onboarding College Professors

Jeffrey L. Buller

With a Foreword by
Stephen Joel Trachtenberg

ROWMAN & LITTLEFIELD
Lanham • Boulder • New York • London

Published by Rowman & Littlefield
A wholly owned subsidiary of The Rowman & Littlefield Publishing Group, Inc.
4501 Forbes Boulevard, Suite 200, Lanham, Maryland 20706
www.rowman.com

Unit A, Whitacre Mews, 26–34 Stannary Street, London SE11 4AB

Copyright © 2017 by Jeffrey L. Buller

All rights reserved. No part of this book may be reproduced in any form or by any
electronic or mechanical means, including information storage and retrieval systems,
without written permission from the publisher, except by a reviewer who may quote
passages in a review.

British Library Cataloguing in Publication Information Available

Library of Congress Cataloging-in-Publication Data Available

ISBN: 978-1-4758-3651-6 (cloth : alk. paper)
ISBN: 978-1-4758-3652-3 (pbk. : alk. paper)
ISBN: 978-1-4758-3653-0 (electronic)

♾™ The paper used in this publication meets the minimum requirements of
American National Standard for Information Sciences—Permanence of Paper
for Printed Library Materials, ANSI/NISO Z39.48–1992.

Printed in the United States of America

To my wife, Sandra, for more than twenty years of love and support.

Contents

Foreword

Ten years ago, when I stepped up after thirty years as a university president at two institutions and sat down as a professor at the George Washington University (GW), I also began an association with Korn Ferry International, one of the world's largest executive search firms, to assist them with their higher education practice. As a dean, president, and a professional consultant, I've hired hundreds of faculty, dozens of deans, vice presidents, and college presidents. My conclusion after a decade of searches is that head hunting is more of an art than a science.

There are, of course, tricks of the trade when conducting faculty searches, as there are with all human activities, but in the end the best searcher is somebody who understands the business, has a capacity to both listen and hear, and has an instinct for putting people together. The theme song for all searches comes to us from *Fiddler on the Roof*, "Matchmaker, Matchmaker, Make Me a Match."

The day after my successor was named at GW, a member of my board of trustees took me aside to congratulate me and to say how proud I must be at the quality of the person they identified to follow me. I was most satisfied but curious as to his exact meaning. I prompted him to go on and he said, "Well, when we recruited you, we got the president of the University of Hartford. The man who follows you is the provost at Johns Hopkins University. This is a testimony to what a great job you have done during your tenure." I know he meant to be complimentary, but I was somewhat off put. I replied, perhaps unkindly, "I would have been more impressed if once again you had recruited the president of the University of Hartford."

Faculty search committees or boards of trustees frequently think they have achieved something consequential if their newly appointed faculty colleague or university president has been recruited from a brand-name institution. The assumption is that somebody who has earned his or her doctorate or has been on the staff at Columbia or Yale inevitably brings a quiver of talents and aptitudes or at least a halo to wherever he or she is going from Manhattan or New Haven. And this is surely sometimes true, but not inevitably.

Because someone's dissertation advisor won the Nobel Prize, the applicant may or may not be a stellar teacher or researcher. Or, not infrequently, the skill set that served an administrator well at a large well-endowed research university is not what is needed at a less affluent, aspiring scrappy institution. Knowing how to do much with little is not an aptitude called upon daily at Harvard.

When one looks at search committees at many universities, they are frequently composed of a Noah's Ark of stakeholders, two by two by gender, race, and national origin: trustees and faculty members, students and community members, alumni and staff people, all of whom—like the sightless men who try to describe an elephant based on touch in the Sufi tale—perceive the elephant as being the one part they can feel. "An elephant is like a snake," says the one who has his hand on the trunk. "An elephant is like a wall," says the one who has his hand on the flank. "An elephant is like a tree," says the one who has his hand on the leg. "An elephant is like a leaf," says the one who has his hand on the ear. The elephant, as of course you and I know, is like a spear because we have our hands on the tusk.

There are ways we can do better, and so here are a few rules of the road I recommend administrators to follow in faculty searches:

- Do not recommend your best friend for the job, no matter how talented she may be. If she doesn't get the job, she'll blame you forever, and if she does get the job, the relationship between you and her will be forever altered because she'll feel beholden.
- The most personable person you interview, the one you'd most like to have dinner with, is not necessarily the individual best suited for the job. Remember the task at hand and put such personal considerations aside. You are not looking for a pal.
- Learn how to read résumés and peer into the paper to find the soul of the candidates and the motivating characteristics for why they might want the job. For example, there are people in their early fifties who are at great universities in the west, but they were born in the east and their parents are now in their mid-late seventies. The candidates are ready to come home, be nearer their aging family, and will sacrifice prestige for personal matters.
- Understand your assignment. An English professor in Texas decided he'd like to move east. Although a full professor and former chair of his department, he applied for a more junior position at Princeton. The

committee chose not to even interview him. Surprised by their inaction he called the chair of the search committee and learned that the committee felt the candidate was overqualified for the post. "Why didn't you tell me that?" he responded. "I would have promised not to tell the students everything I know."

In addition, search committees run the risk of having a dour outcome at the end of a successful process. Two possible scenarios:

1. At the end of a round of interviews, the chair takes a straw poll and asks the members to rank the interviewees. There is no majority consensus for any particular "number one" candidate; however, almost everyone on the committee agrees on "number two." That person is offered and accepts the position. Many on the committee walk away believing it would have been better had someone else had come out on top. They are used to winning, not settling.
2. The committee agrees on a finalist, and the chair begins negotiations to engage the successful candidate. After a short period of back and forth, the candidate withdraws from consideration, deciding for personal reasons to remain at his or her present institution. The committee quickly regroups and offers the job to the runner-up, a very capable person. Once again the committee sulks at not reeling in their first choice. Rather than being happy about a successful rebound, they dwell on the missed shot.

We should remember that timing, chance, opportunity, chemistry, luck, and happenstance all play a role in a search committee's selection process. That said, there are clear best practices and techniques that professionalize the process, ensuring it works fairly, smoothly, in a collegiate manner and reaches a conclusion that engages new talent for a campus.

To benefit from Jeff Buller's experience in conducting more than thirty years of faculty searches, read his book. You'll enjoy it, and you'll be wiser when you finish than when you begin.

— Stephen Joel Trachtenberg

Stephen Joel Trachtenberg is president emeritus and university professor at the George Washington University. He is a consultant at Korn Ferry International and Rimon Law and coeditor of *Presidencies Derailed: Why University Leaders Fail and How to Prevent It* (Baltimore, MD: Johns Hopkins University Press, 2013).

Preface

F. Scott Fitzgerald's short story "The Rich Boy" includes the famous passage, "Let me tell you about the very rich. They are different from you and me" (Fitzgerald 1926, 1), to which Ernest Hemingway later gave a famous answer in a short story of his own by saying, "Yes, they have more money" (Hemingway 1977, 76). Well, it really doesn't matter much whether you agree with Fitzgerald or Hemingway about how similar *you and I* may be to the very rich. But I do believe that there's a truth we need to recognize about institutions: The very rich ones are different from yours and mine.

The Harvards, Yales, and Princetons of the world have all the resources and clout they need to attract the most accomplished and distinguished professors. At lower ranks, they can hire as many graduates as they like from top-ranked programs, set the bar extremely high for what they expect from these faculty members in terms of their teaching and research, offer tenure to few (if any) of them six years later, and then begin the process all over again.

Most colleges and universities aren't like that. The chance to hire a faculty member on tenure track or with a multiyear appointment doesn't occur as often as we'd like, particularly in difficult economic times. So, if you're the one making the decision about whom to hire, you have to get it right. You're literally making a multimillion-dollar investment when you figure in the costs involved with the search itself, any start-up funding that may be required, and the total income and benefits that will be paid to the faculty member over the course of his or her career.

In most recruitment and hiring processes, you're not just trying to find a new coworker; you're trying to identify someone who'll become a good colleague, a person who can make the difference between an environment you look forward to rejoining each day and one that leaves you counting the days until your retirement.

This book is written for those who are commonly called hiring authorities—the people who make the decisions about whom to hire and who often negotiate the offer themselves—at institutions that do not qualify as "very rich." At these schools, there are almost certainly policies already in place that outline what you must, can, and cannot do during a faculty search. But although what's necessary and possible may be well recorded, the tips and insights that constitute *best practices* are passed down only as part of a school's oral tradition.

You may be reading this book because you're chairing your first search, trying to avoid some of the mistakes you made during your last search, interested in picking up a few pointers that have helped other department chairs and deans, or hoping to get the next hire right simply because you're dedicated to your job. This book is intended for all of you.

We're going to consider practices that academic leaders have taken at colleges and universities just like yours in their own efforts to recruit and hire new faculty members. So, if you're the sort of person who looks at a faculty search as not a burden to wrap up as quickly as possible but an opportunity to build your program and make your institution even better than it is right now, you've come to exactly the right place.

Designing or realigning faculty positions, choosing the best candidate, and negotiating the final offer are among the most important responsibilities we have as academic leaders. But the end result—a new colleague who can help our programs and institutions improve and possibly become another academic leader in turn—makes all that effort worthwhile. I wish you nothing but the best in your own searches, and I hope to hear of your successes in putting these ideas into practice.

Jeffrey L. Buller
Jupiter, Florida
January 15, 2017
jbuller@atlasleadership.com

Acknowledgments

I'd like to express my gratitude to Rebecca Peter for editorial assistance, Sandy Ogden for stylistic advice, Selene Vazquez for research assistance, and Stephen Joel Trachtenberg for his generosity in providing his insights in the foreword. All four of these wonderful friends played a significant role in making this book better than it otherwise would have been.

Introduction

The intended audience of this book consists of what are often called *hiring authorities*, the people who make the actual decision about whether to offer a contract to a particular candidate. In most cases, that means that you're a dean or a department chair and that you thus have one of the most important responsibilities in higher education: choosing the people who will join your faculty and help advance your school's mission of teaching, research, and service.

If you make the right decision, a program can thrive, bring credit to the entire institution, and (let's be frank about it) make your own job a lot easier. If you make the wrong decision, even a single person can bring the progress of a formerly successful program to a crashing halt and complicate your job enormously. So, you have both professional and selfish reasons to make sure that you're hiring the right person.

In order to make *Hire the Right Faculty Member Every Time* useful to both individual readers and participants in a workshop on faculty hiring, I've formatted a number of passages in particular ways:

> **Passages that are formatted in this way are concise summaries of the best practices referred to in the book's title. They've been set apart like this so that they'll be easy for you to find again when you've finished reading this book or for others to find when they're just flipping through the pages.**

In addition, there are a few passages in chapters 2 and 6 that are formatted as follows:

These passages are thought experiments. They're opportunities for you to pause for a moment and imagine how you might respond in the situation presented. They're designed to help you *experience* an insight rather than merely be *told* a bit of information. Thought experiments provide vivid and memorable illustrations of key ideas in the text. If you're leading a workshop on faculty searches, these passages make good exercises.

I've written another book, *Best Practices for Faculty Search Committees: How to Review Applications and Interview Candidates* (Jossey-Bass, 2017), for members of the faculty, staff, and administration who will assist you in your search. If they need guidance, please refer them to that work. In the volume you're holding right now, we'll be focusing exclusively on the sorts of things that are beneficial to people like yourself, those who make hiring decisions—and who then have to live with the consequences. Since that's what's at stake in your choices of whom to hire, turn the page and let's get started on a systematic approach to getting it right.

Chapter 1

Understanding Faculty Searches Today

Back in the 1970s, the college professor who eventually became my mentor and best academic role model got his job this way: When he was almost done with his dissertation, his advisor made some calls to a few friends, found that they were in need of a new classicist at the University of Notre Dame, and told the department chair there, "You need to hire this guy." That was it.

Now, when you read that story, your reaction is probably either to cringe at the inadequacies of the "old boys network" (and then rejoice that such an antiquated system is gone) or to feel wistful longing for the "good old days" (and then experience a wave of nostalgia for their passing). In any case, searching and recruiting faculty members today isn't what it used to be.

It's now a prolonged, complex, and *very* expensive proposition. It can also feel a bit like a shot in the dark: Even if you do everything right, there's still a chance that the person you hire won't work out and that you'll be doing it all over again in a year's time.

Is there anything we can do to make the process of recruiting and hiring faculty members a little more efficient and, at the same time, increase our likelihood for success? If we want to get to a better place in our practice of conducting searches, it's helpful to understand where we are right now.

What do faculty searches look like at other colleges and universities similar to our own? Are there any best practices we can borrow from what some institutions are doing to improve our own handling of searches? Do some schools with budgets as limited as our own have a better track record of hiring faculty members who succeed in their environments?

In order to answer some of these questions, Robert E. Cipriano (my partner in ATLAS: Academic Training, Leadership, & Assessment Services) and

I decided to survey 638 faculty members and administrators at a broad range of schools across North America and ask them about their search practices. We were particularly interested in whether they were satisfied with how they recruit and hire new colleagues, how faculty searches might differ from staff or administrative searches, what activities tended to be included during on-campus interview visits, whether the composition of search committees varied according to the level of position (e.g., entry-level assistant professor versus senior scholar), and what problems they tended to encounter during faculty searches.

PROBLEMS AND AREAS OF DISSATISFACTION WITH RECRUITMENT AND HIRING

On the whole, those who participated in the survey were satisfied with the way in which faculty searches are being conducted at their institutions but significantly less satisfied with the hiring process that occurred at the end of a search. When asked "In general, how satisfied are you with your institution's current procedure for recruiting faculty members? (*recruiting* for the sake of this question means the process of advertising a position and soliciting applications)," participants responded in the following ways:

- 1.2% were completely satisfied.
- 58.3% were rather satisfied.
- 21.2% were neither satisfied nor dissatisfied.
- 16.6% were rather dissatisfied.
- 2.7% were completely dissatisfied.

But when the question became "In general, how satisfied are you with your institution's current procedure for hiring faculty members? (*hiring* for the sake of this question means the process of selecting the successful candidate, offering the position, and having the offer accepted)," that level of satisfaction dropped precipitously:

- 0.6% claimed to be completely satisfied.
- 18.3% reported that they were rather satisfied.
- 8.8% described themselves as neither satisfied nor dissatisfied.
- 52.4% said they were rather dissatisfied.
- 19.9% called themselves completely dissatisfied.

What happens between the recruitment stage of a search and the hiring stage that accounts for this dramatic difference?

The comments made by those participating in the survey provide us with some answers. The faculty members we contacted (76.5% of participants, with the remaining 23.5% describing themselves as either administrators or staff members) felt that they themselves had a great deal of control over the recruitment process. They decided what qualifications their new colleagues should have, asked the questions in interviews that they wanted answered, and recommended the finalist whom they regarded as the best match for their needs.

But that control vanished, at least in their perception of the process, once they passed on their recommendations to an administrator. They felt that their recommendations were sometimes ignored or that the administrator didn't pursue a highly desirable candidate as aggressively as the faculty wanted. Some participants described their dissatisfaction in the following ways:

- "Faculty colleagues/peers are in the best position to know the needs of their department. If faculty are forced to hire a person because the dean selected that candidate, it will be a nightmare."
- "When the dean makes the decision whom to hire in our department, it is usually a mess."
- "If the provost is interested in a particular candidate (for whatever reason), anything seems possible: The salary becomes negotiable; start-up funds are suddenly available; new offices appear (constructed out of classrooms, if necessary). But if we in the department want some flexibility in the offer we can make someone, the budget magically becomes too tight for any accommodation."

Similar sentiments were echoed when people were asked what one thing they would change about faculty searches if they could:

- "The search committee should make the decision to hire a faculty colleague rather than the dean or another administrator."
- "The faculty/search committee should be given the final say in which candidate is hired."
- "Our institution needs to do a better job of advertising nationally for its searches. As it is, the assumption is that we will be hiring someone from our local region and ideally someone who has a degree from our own institution. As a result, we sometimes don't have an opportunity to recruit the best candidates available."
- "Greater resources need to be devoted to the recruitment and hiring processes. For example, we don't have any budget established for reimbursing faculty who are moving to the region to accept a position. All such reimbursements must come from our operating budgets. We've lost good candidates over this."

Because of these concerns, the inability of those taking the survey to attract and hire the best candidates for a position was a major concern. A full 81.8% of respondents could remember a search in which none of the viable candidates was willing to accept an offer once it was made, and a little more than two-thirds (68.4%) knew of a candidate who had to be let go after less than a year on the job. Even though respondents were, as we saw, largely satisfied with the search processes at their own colleges and universities, they were candid about some of the problems they saw when trying to identify candidates who fit their greatest needs:

- 82.3% had been involved in a search where there was insufficient ethnic diversity in the candidate pool.
- 81.4% had seen insufficient ethnic diversity on the search committee itself.
- 52.6% had encountered insufficient gender diversity on a search committee.
- 29.9% had experienced insufficient gender diversity in a candidate pool.
- 53.5% could recall a candidate who, after he or she was hired, seemed to have a very different personality from the one he or she demonstrated during the interview.
- 41.1% could recall a candidate who, after he or she was hired, did not have the skill set or experience he or she claimed during the interview.
- 28.3% knew of a candidate who accepted the position but later reneged on his or her acceptance.
- 27.6% had encountered a candidate who agreed during the interviews to teach certain courses but, once hired, refused to teach those courses.
- 15.1% were aware of incidents when a candidate accepted the position but simply did not show up when his or her contract began.
- 12.8% could recall a candidate who blatantly lied on his or her curriculum vitae.

THE USE OF PROFESSIONAL SEARCH FIRMS AND TECHNOLOGY

With widespread changes in technology and the availability of professional services to assist with the search process, we also wanted to know how the process of selecting and interviewing candidates had changed over the past fifty years. Unfortunately, the answer we received over and over again was that it had changed less than we had hoped.

For example, even though professional search firms, which can help institutions broaden their pools of qualified candidates and ensure that all appropriate policies are scrupulously followed, are much more common today than they were a few decades ago, these firms are still used almost exclusively for administrative, rather than faculty, searches:

- Virtually no one among those participating in our survey (indeed, only one respondent out of the 638 people we contacted) had ever known search firms to be used regularly for faculty positions.
- On the other hand, 81.3% said that their institutions were likely to use a search firm when hiring a president or chancellor.
- An even larger majority, 84.8%, said that their institutions would do so when searching for a new provost.
- 52.4% said search firms were commonly used in searching for a dean.
- Only 5.7% said that search firms were common when hiring a department chair.

Perhaps the biggest surprise in these results is that institutions were more likely to use a search firm when hiring a provost than a president or chancellor. One possible explanation is that the school's governing board, a body that usually includes many members with corporate or political backgrounds, commonly conducts these presidential searches. These boards, particularly at smaller schools, may feel that they already have sufficient expertise to conduct an effective search independently and thus choose to forgo the expense of working with a search firm.

The president, on the other hand, typically leads searches for provosts. Particularly in the case of people who are in their first presidencies, a new CEO may not feel that he or she has sufficient experience or time to conduct a suitably ambitious search for a provost. As a result, the president may welcome turning part of the process over to a professional search firm that may be able to attract and prescreen a better pool of qualified applicants.

In a similar way, although "airport interviews"—medium-length interviews (usually one to three hours) held either in an airport conference room or in a nearby hotel—are sometimes used when institutions are hiring new members of the upper administration, this practice is underutilized in faculty searches:

- 31.1% of those participating in the survey didn't believe that airport interviews were ever used at their institution for either faculty or administrative searches.
- 63.2% of respondents reported that airport interviews may be used for certain administrative positions but not for faculty positions.
- Only 5.7% were aware of cases in which faculty searches included an airport interview, and several of those respondents noted that this practice occurred only for senior positions, such as in searches for a distinguished professor or eminent scholar.

Finally, the use of technology is still relatively limited in faculty searches. Videoconferencing may have replaced or supplemented telephone interviews at many schools—77.3% of respondents had participated in a search where candidates were contacted by Skype, FaceTime, or similar technology as part of an initial screening process—but the tradition of bringing candidates to campus for interviews is alive and well.

The only cases participants could recall of a videoconference *replacing* an in-person interview were rare situations in which severe weather interfered with candidate travel or where the faculty member was being recruited abroad solely to teach online courses. In all other cases, even where distance learning was a major part of the faculty members' responsibilities, the search committees still chose to incur the expense of meeting applicants in person.

THE COMPOSITION OF SEARCH COMMITTEES

If search firms aren't involved in the vast majority of searches for faculty members, who is? It turns out that the answer to this question varies quite a bit depending on the type and level of position that are involved. For example, here are the results people gave when they were asked whether they would ordinarily expect representation to be there on the search committee from various groups when there was a search for an entry-level assistant professor:

- 94.6% expected to find full professors on such a committee.
- 86.1% expected associate professors to be involved.
- 75.3% expected to see assistant professors.
- 70.4% expected the department chair to be involved.
- 29.7% expected the committee to include current students.
- 21.1% expected to find current instructors, lecturers, or other non-ranked faculty members on the committee.
- 15.8% expected the dean to be represented.
- 9.9% expected staff members from human resources to be present.
- 4.7% expected alumni to be there.

Several other interesting results from this part of the survey are the following:

- By far, the most common constituency groups to be present on a search committee were tenure-eligible faculty members, including the department chair. All other groups were commonly represented at less than one-third of the institutions we surveyed.

- Students were nearly twice as likely to be represented on the search committee as the dean.
- Even though they were not eligible for tenure, instructors and lecturers were still more commonly represented on search committees for assistant professors than was the dean.
- Staff members from human resources are not commonly represented on faculty search committees. At most institutions, there is a fairly clear division between the hiring of faculty members (largely run out of the provost's office, with the office of human resources only becoming involved once the candidate is chosen) and staff members (largely run out of the office of human resources).

When the question shifted to search committees for a senior or distinguished professor, the groups likely to be represented on search committees changed somewhat. The following are the percentages of respondents to the survey who expected each of the following groups to be represented on such a search committee:

- 98.3: full professors
- 81.2: associate professors
- 78.7: the department chair
- 60.3: assistant professors
- 45.4: the dean
- 15.2: current instructors, lecturers, or other non-ranked faculty members
- 15.1: current students
- 14.6: emeritus faculty members
- 11.0: staff members from human resources
- 10.4: administrators with a higher rank than dean
- 9.8: alumni
- 5.7: members of a governing board
- 4.6: members of an advisory board

At this level of employment, it's almost certain that the search committee will include full professors, with there being a high likelihood of other tenure-eligible faculty members, the chair, and the dean also being represented. These senior positions also occasionally involve the participation of alumni, various types of boards, upper administrators, and emeritus faculty members, all groups that none of the respondents reported as involved in searches for entry-level assistant professors.

Very similar results occurred when we asked about national searches for a department chair. The one change was that nontenure-eligible faculty members were somewhat more likely to be involved in this type of search. Here are the percentages of respondents who reported that they would expect to see the following groups represented on a national search for a new department head:

- 97.2: full professors
- 89.9: chairs from other departments
- 81.6: associate professors
- 66.2: assistant professors
- 55.6: the dean
- 35.0: current instructors, lecturers, or other non-ranked faculty members
- 31.3: current, outgoing, or former chairs (from the same department)
- 25.7: current students
- 24.3: administrators with a higher rank than dean
- 15.1: members of an advisory board
- 9.7: staff members from human resources
- 4.4: alumni

The type of search that tended to include the broadest range of stakeholder groups was a search for a senior administrator, such as a president or provost. In this case, eleven of the fourteen groups we asked about could be expected to have representations on the search committees at more than a third of our respondents' institutions:

- 91.1%: full professors
- 85.0%: deans
- 76.7%: administrators with a higher rank than dean
- 71.8%: department chairs
- 60.6%: associate professors
- 55.1%: staff members from human resources
- 50.2%: nonacademic vice presidents
- 45.5%: assistant professors
- 41.3%: members of an advisory board
- 39.8%: current students
- 35.5%: alumni
- 29.6%: members of a faculty union
- 20.2%: current instructors, lecturers, or other non-ranked faculty members
- 10.3%: emeritus faculty members

A "TYPICAL" FACULTY INTERVIEW PROCESS

Next, we wanted to learn what activities these participants engaged in with candidates during the interview process. We began by asking how many candidates were brought to campus for interviews during a typical faculty search.

The vast majority of respondents (93.1%) reported that inviting three finalists was the norm. A small group of schools (5.7%), all small private colleges, reported that they usually interviewed two applicants and proceeded to a third or a fourth only when a suitable candidate couldn't be found among the initial group. The remaining schools (1.2%) said that either there was no set number of finalists they could interview or it was "however many we can justify to the dean."

But even though there was a great deal of consistency about the number of candidates who were brought to campus for interviews, there was, as might be expected, very little consistency in the number of applicants who were included in the entire pool. The range of applicants in a "typical" faculty search in the survey participants' own departments or programs ranged from a low of 15 to a high of 300, with a median of 75 and an average of 92.5.

Factors that correlated with smaller applicant pools were institutions enrolling 3,000 or fewer students, departments that offered professional degrees, and schools that had a predominantly undergraduate mission. Factors that correlated with larger applicant pools were institutions enrolling 20,000 or more students, departments that offered degrees in the liberal arts and sciences, and schools that had a comprehensive or research mission.

We next wanted to know how long most campus interviews would last during faculty searches:

- 41.1% of our respondents said that interviews for prospective faculty members typically lasted a day and a half at their institutions.
- 39.2% said they usually lasted one day.
- 11.6% said that faculty interviews usually lasted for two days.
- 5.3% said they were often over in less than a day.
- 2.8% said they lasted for more than two days.

As for the activities usually included in those on-campus interviews, most people said that the most common events arranged for candidates were question-and-answer sessions with various stakeholder groups:

- 100% of the respondents said that these interviews included in-person meetings with the search committee. In fact, one could almost define an on-campus interview as a conversation with a search committee that may also include one or more of the activities mentioned in all the bullet points below.
- 92.4% said that candidates usually had one-on-one meetings with the department chair.
- 88.3% said that candidates met with the dean.

- 86.4% said that a complete interview process included telephone calls to references.
- 85.7% of respondents said that their institutions conducted telephone interviews with the candidates before inviting them to campus. A few also noted in the comments that they may conduct additional telephone interviews after the campus visit if there were unresolved questions.
- 83.0% said that meals during the campus visit were generally considered part of the interview process.
- 65.8% said their institutions built in specially designated rest time for the candidates.
- 64.7% said that candidates gave research-focused "job talks."
- 55.2% said their interviews included in-person meetings with faculty members who were not on the search committee.
- 51.8% said that candidates were expected to teach a section of an actual course.
- 50.3% noted that interviews often included special opportunities for students to meet with the candidate and ask questions.
- 47.3% said that candidates often taught a "pseudo-course" (e.g., a sample class taught before faculty members, a select group of students, or other activities that were similar to a class but not scheduled as part of a regular course).
- 42.9% said that open meetings with mixed groups of stakeholders were common.
- 35.8% said that the interview process usually included tours of the community with someone other than a realtor.
- 31.5% said that interviews included one-on-one meetings with the provost.
- 26.7% said that interviews included specially designated sections for staff members.
- 23.2% reported that interviews often included one-on-one meetings between the candidate and the chair of the search committee.
- 21.1% said that their schools often provided the candidates with tours of the community conducted by a realtor.
- 8.6% said that candidates regularly met one-on-one with the president.
- Only 1.4% said that candidates often had meetings with alumni.

That's a fairly large number of activities to fit into a process that, as we saw, was usually over in less than two days. No search process will have time to include everything we asked about on our survey. Committees will select various activities based on past practice, the mission of the school or program, the desire of individual administrators or committee members, and the level of the position.

At very small schools, it is relatively easy for every faculty candidate to have a courtesy meeting with the president, provost, and dean. At larger schools, those meetings may occur only for very senior positions or the most prestigious of candidates.

PUTTING IT ALL TOGETHER

Despite everything we can do to help make the faculty search process fairer and more systematic, recruitment of faculty will always remain more an art than a science. It is an intensely human process, and humans make mistakes.

Members of a search committee can make an unconscious decision almost instantaneously because they don't like how an applicant has structured a letter of interest, used a font that strikes them as unattractive, reminded them of a colleague from their past, or not shaken hands as firmly as they would like. We'll never be able to eliminate all of those human factors, and we wouldn't want to.

In higher education, we often spend more hours each day with our colleagues than with our families, and we want to hire people we can imagine ourselves working with for the long term. When that desire moves us toward finding the most collegial, professional, and supportive applicants we can find, it's highly commendable. When that desire moves us toward hiring only other people who look, think, and work exactly like us, it can lead to a program that's stagnant and excessively homogeneous.

In the following chapters, therefore, we want to examine practices that colleges and universities have found helpful in making hiring decisions in the right way and for the right reason. Since, as we saw in this chapter, faculty hiring and recruiting is almost always an internal process and thus almost never turned over to an external search firm, we have an obligation to train our search chairs and committees in how to be more effective in this process. The remainder of this book will explore ways of doing so in order to increase the likelihood that the searches for which you're responsible will have the best possible results.

Chapter 2

Defining the Position

In many ways, properly defining a faculty position is the most important step in the entire process of recruiting and hiring someone. Unfortunately, it's the step that's often given the least attention, with the first question being, "What are we going to put into the ad?" instead of "What sort of person would best fit our needs at this time?"

In order to start thinking more holistically about the search process, let's consider how faculty careers often begin and how some of them end. We'll try to gain a bit of perspective through the following two thought experiments.

THOUGHT EXPERIMENT 2.1: PREPARING FOR A SEARCH

Imagine that you've just been allocated a new faculty position. The line you've been assigned comes with its own funding, and so you now have the ability to hire someone in your discipline with a specialty in whichever area you regard as most important for your program's future success. The problem is that you've received this new position very late in the recruitment cycle, and you need to post an advertisement for it immediately in order to meet a publication deadline.

Because of your other commitments, you don't have time to write the job description yourself. So, you delegate that task to the chair of a search committee you've hastily appointed and give that person a list of the five most important things you believe the search committee should look for in a candidate.

In the spaces below, jot down the five most important credentials, attributes, areas of experience, or personal traits that you believe the

search committee should keep in mind when defining the position, writing the ad, and selecting the best possible candidate for the job.

1. _____
2. _____
3. _____
4. _____
5. _____

Now that we've given some attention to how the process of recruiting a faculty member could *begin*, let's turn next to an exercise that can help us think about how at least a few faculty careers end.

THOUGHT EXPERIMENT 2.2: THE COLLEAGUE WHO DIDN'T WORK OUT

Think of an experience you either had yourself or heard about from someone else when a faculty member who was hired ended up not being successful. Perhaps this person was fired, his or her contract was not renewed, or other people in the program simply endured a bad situation until he or she quit, was assigned elsewhere, or retired. Or perhaps the person is still working with you, but many people are gritting their teeth and making do until this person leaves.

In the space below, answer this question: What went wrong?

_____
_____

Once you've completed these two thought experiments, look at what you wrote in the second exercise about what went wrong and ask yourself this question: Would any of the five things I identified as the *most important things* a search committee should look for in a candidate have prevented what went wrong in Thought Experiment 2.2? Perhaps it would have.

Perhaps a candidate you once hired proved unsuccessful at research once on the job, and so you emphasized to the search committee how important it would be for applicants to better document that he or she has an ongoing and sustainable plan for their research. Or maybe you took a chance on a candidate who hadn't quite finished his or her dissertation but promised that it would be finished "within three months," although it remained incomplete three or four years later. To avoid a recurrence of this problem, perhaps one of your five instructions to the search committee was that each applicant had to have his or her terminal degree *in hand* at the time of application.

In most cases, however, it probably wasn't a matter of credentials or documentation that proved to be the employee's undoing. More likely it was something harder to put your finger on.

The person may have been noncollegial, had an air of entitlement, or refused to do his or her share of the committee work needed to keep your program going. Or the person may have had anger issues, failed to show up for classes for no apparent reason, insisted on teaching a different set of courses from the one he or she was hired to teach, or caused so many problems with other members of the faculty that the situation was no longer tenable.

In most cases, it's interpersonal conflict of some sort that causes a faculty member to fail, but we almost never consider these interpersonal issues when we're defining a position or gearing up for a search. In fact, when it comes to most faculty search processes,

> **We hire people on the basis of what they have accomplished, but people succeed or fail on the basis of how they behave.**

Or to put it another way,

> **We're really good at reading résumés, but we're far less proficient at reading people.**

So, how can we do better? We can start by completely rethinking our process of how we define and build faculty positions as we prepare for a search.

EVERY OPENING IS AN OPPORTUNITY

When vacancies occur, academic departments frequently look at only the possibility for continuity and extension, not improvement and transformation. For example, if a professor retires after having had a teaching and research specialty in X, Y, and Z, the temptation is to fill the position with another person who specializes in X, Y, and Z. And if the new faculty member can do that while also bringing the program experience in W, so much the better.

But that's not the most effective way to conduct a search. Higher education is a rapidly changing enterprise. Our academic fields evolve, new disciplines are created, new generations of students have needs and interests different from those of their predecessors, and new research problems emerge. Similarly, if a program is allocated a new faculty line, most departments decide to make slight, incremental expansions to their curriculum or, worse, shunt all their undesirable courses and responsibilities onto the new person while making their own assignments easier.

The fact of the matter is that, when we use the hiring process merely to find a replacement or create a slight expansion in our program, we're not taking full advantage of what's available to us.

> **Every faculty opening is an opportunity. We should use that opportunity to reexamine where we want our program to go and how we can best get there.**

In other words, instead of thinking, "The professor who's retiring taught X, Y, and Z, so we need to hire a new specialist in X, Y, and Z," we should be asking, "What is our program capable of becoming in the next five to ten years, and what sort of credentials, attributes, areas of experience, and personal traits will be needed to get us there?"

Just as zero-base budgeting reevaluates the funding allocated to each program from scratch every fiscal year in order to make sure that the institution's highest priorities are properly addressed, so should we engage in what one might call zero-base faculty recruitment. With zero-base faculty recruitment, a program would list all its needs in one column of a document and its potential assets in another column of the document. By trying to foresee what may be possible for the program five to ten years out, people will be encouraged to look beyond immediate needs and concerns and to what could help the program achieve its fullest potential.

When conducting this exercise, the group should try to keep its frame of reference to no more than five or ten years in the future, as anything beyond that probably won't be very helpful, and other additions to, and departures from, the program will change the area's needs even further. The discipline and student body will continue to evolve over that time, and unpredictable economic or political factors may make the landscape for higher education completely unrecognizable a dozen or more years from now. In order to be the best program realistically possible within a five- to ten-year window, the department can ask questions like the following:

- What courses will we need in our curriculum?
- What credentials will be necessary to teach those courses?
- How often will each course in that curriculum need to be taught?
- Which research areas best complement or build on those that currently exist in the program?
- What service assignments will the program probably be responsible for?
- What levels of diversity will provide the richest environment for teaching and research?
- In which areas of diversity have we consistently lagged behind what our targets should be?
- What would an appropriately diverse faculty look like?
- What skills and areas of experience are most needed to accomplish the work of the department, college or division, and institution?
- What would we need in order to say that we have transformed ourselves in a positive way?

Once all these needs and desires are summarized in the first column of the document—which by now could easily be many pages long—it's time to start the second column that lists the assets your program is likely to have in five to ten years. While taking into account the current members of the department who are likely to retire, move into the administration, or leave their faculty positions for any other reason, the department should consider which members will still be on faculty in five to ten years and ask the following questions:

- Which of them has appropriate credentials to teach which courses (existing, anticipated, or desired)?
- What research specialties does each person have?
- What service strengths and interests does each person have?
- What kind of diversity does each person bring?
- In which areas of diversity have we consistently lagged behind what our targets should be?
- What skills and areas of experience does each person have (aside from his or her academic credentials)?
- What other qualities or attributes does each person have?

Once all the program's anticipated needs and desires have been listed in one column and all its assets have been listed in another, the next step is to match the items from the two columns. Certain faculty members and other resources will be capable of meeting many of the identified needs, but there will still probably be a large number of needs and desires left over. Those items that remain unaccounted for among the current assets can guide the department in how best to design the next several positions it fills in the program.

By having identified the number of sections of various courses that you'll need, you may discover that, even though the program currently has faculty members with credentials to teach those courses, there aren't enough people to staff all the sections you need. You may discover that some needs are better addressed by changing the assignments of current faculty members than by seeking a full-time specialist in that area. And you may find that, as pressing as the need once seemed to offer electives in a new specialty, a bigger concern for the program might be to diversify the faculty by bringing in highly qualified faculty members who broaden your program's representation in terms of gender, ethnicity, sexual orientation, or other protected classes at your institution.

"That all may be well and good," someone might say, "but we have classes that we have to offer. I need to staff a program. I can't waste time worrying about what might or might not be the case five or ten years from now." Certainly, as academic leaders, we all have obligations to address our immediate needs, but the advantage that zero-base faculty recruitment brings is that it gives us an opportunity to pull back from these immediate needs for a moment and ask ourselves what is necessary and *what only seems necessary.*

In other words, we may think that we need a professor who can teach intermediate hydroponic cryptography because, according to our curriculum, that course is a prerequisite to the seminar on advanced subsonic conspiracy theory, which is required of all majors. But those requirements may have been set because of the nature of the discipline several years ago, or because they may still reflect the research interests of the faculty members who designed the program a decade ago. The questions really should be more like the following:

- What curricular areas make sense for our discipline now and will continue to make sense five or ten years in the future?
- Are all the prerequisites we have in place truly essential in order to succeed at later courses?
- Could a broader range of options make it easier for students to build a schedule that works for them at the same time that it provides them with the knowledge and skills our discipline now regards as important?
- By rethinking our program, could we open the way for new developments and the type of growth that can benefit our stakeholders more in the future?

STRATEGIC HIRING

Another way of thinking more creatively about faculty positions is the approach known as strategic hiring or cluster hiring. With strategic hiring, the goal is not merely to fill the needs of an individual program but also to develop a corps of faculty in important areas that can help establish or develop specific institutional strengths. This method allows for a university to hire a group of faculty members from complementary academic disciplines or specialties in a way that builds an interdisciplinary center of excellence in a field that the institution regards as vital to its development.

Which fields are appropriate for strategic hiring? That question is difficult to answer universally because it's so dependent on institutional mission. In most cases, however, a good place to begin looking for guidance about where this method may be appropriate is your institution's strategic plan.

Most institutional strategic plans either explicitly address or implicitly suggest that the school has certain pillars and platforms that it regards as key to its identity. Pillars (sometimes referred to as pillars of excellence or, at Christian schools, steeples of excellence) are those programs that are widely recognized to be among the school's best and most distinctive offerings.

Sometimes pillars are found within particular departments, such as a college of business administration with an accounting program that places 100% of its graduates into jobs at prestigious firms immediately after graduation, but pillars may also transcend individual programs by capitalizing on the strengths these programs achieve by working together. Examples of suitable interdisciplinary pillars might include the following:

- nanotechnology
- neuroscience
- bioimaging
- sustainable urban development
- human aging
- biomedical engineering
- digital media studies
- agroecology
- medical ethics
- poverty studies

Strategic hiring in these areas would consist of recruiting a team of faculty members from different disciplines who have research specialties closely related to the theme of the pillar.

An institution might decide to establish a pillar from scratch ("As we look toward the future, it's clear that sustainable urban development is going to be a major challenge for our region. Currently, none of the universities in this region—including us—offers such a program. So, let's make it a priority this year to hire a team of faculty members with a research emphasis in sustainable urban development as we make our hires in such areas as urban planning, architecture, sociology, environmental studies, medicine. . . .") or by augmenting existing strengths ("We have some very strong faculty members in the fields of biology, psychology, and nursing who work in the area of human aging. We could achieve national prominence in this area if we hired some additional scholars who work in the field of aging in such disciplines as economics, education, physical therapy, engineering. . . .").

In addition to pillars of excellence, some strategic plans also provide insight into the school's platforms: foundations of strength that cut across all its programs. Unlike pillars that bring together prominent aspects of only a few key disciplines, platforms represent the forms of distinction that the institution has identified in every academic program it offers (and possibly even in some nonacademic units of the institution). Examples of common institutional platforms include the following:

- undergraduate research
- leadership development
- community service
- diversity
- innovation, creativity, and entrepreneurship
- development of critical thinking
- excellence in oral and written communication
- community engagement
- globalization
- personalization

For example, an institution might build its strengths on the platform of personalization if all its academic programs could be adapted to fit the individual needs, interests, and schedule of each individual student. Likewise, it could build on the platform of leadership development if not only academic programs but also student life, human resources, athletics, and advancement made it a priority to help everyone they serve grow in his or her leadership potential.

The advantage of strategic hiring is that it leverages the strengths of different areas of the institution in such a way that the school's identity becomes more distinctive in an increasingly crowded educational marketplace. Prospective students, donors, employers, and community partners will know more readily what the school does besides engaging in teaching, research, and service—the activities performed by every other postsecondary institution in the world.

Many institutions believe that it's better to be known as "the best college in the region for nanotechnology and undergraduate research" than as just "a pretty good school" across the board. But all the strategic planning in the world can't help a school develop that distinctive identity if it keeps hiring new faculty members in the same way it always has. Building areas of strength requires collective effort, from the president or chancellor all the way down to members of individual search committees, all of whom regard strategic hiring as important and incorporate it into the way they define faculty positions.

Some faculty resistance to strategic hiring may occur if it addresses only pillars that include a limited number of disciplines. By making certain areas pillars of excellence, it can cause people in other fields to wonder, "What are the rest of us then? Valleys of mediocrity?"

In order to avoid this potential challenge to morale, it's a good practice to select three to five institutional pillars of excellence that, as a group, include representation from as broad an array of disciplines as possible. Then the college or university should complement those pillars with roughly the same number of platforms. Since platforms, by definition, cut across all the programs at the institution, they provide an effective way of demonstrating that, regardless of how strategic the hiring process will be at the institution, it will still provide an opportunity for all disciplines to participate.

CAUTIONS WHEN DESIGNING POSITIONS

One of the mistakes academic programs often commit when preparing for a faculty search is defining a position too narrowly. You can decrease your likelihood of making this mistake if you take zero-base faculty recruitment and strategic hiring seriously.

But you can't guarantee that your search committee won't lapse into old habits as the process gets under way. After all, the list of unmet needs that you'll probably produce when you engage in zero-base faculty recruitment and possibilities you can imagine when you engage in strategic hiring is probably quite long. If you add to those lists the elements of diversity, collegiality, and other highly desirable contributions the new faculty member could bring to the program, you could easily end up with a set of desired qualities that no one on earth could possibly have.

Positions are rarely defined so narrowly that no one at all can meet the qualifications, but they're often defined in such a way that candidates who could bring great benefits to the program are inadvertently excluded. In order to explore this idea further, let's engage in the following thought experiment.

THOUGHT EXPERIMENT 2.3: TOO MANY DESIRES

Overly Specialized State University has a strategic plan that calls for the institution to launch a new program in transnational prenuptial agreement studies. As part of its strategic hiring plan, the Department of Thirteenth-Century Flemish Economic Analysis wants to hire a new historian of Flemish economics with a specialty in Medieval and Renaissance European prenuptial agreements.

The department has engaged in a zero-base faculty recruitment process and developed the following list of qualifications and attributes it aims to find in its new faculty member. It is hoped that the new member of the department will bring the following qualities to the program:

- the ability to teach TCFE 1001: Introduction to Thirteenth-Century Flemish Economic Analysis, TCFE 4032: Proseminar in Thirteenth-Century Flemish Economic Analysis, and TCFE 4088: Medieval and Renaissance Flemish Prenuptial Agreements
- gender diversity, since the department currently consists of fifteen men and only one woman
- ethnic diversity, since all the members of the program are currently Belgians
- experience in strategic planning
- familiarity with accreditation by both the university's regional accrediting body and the department's disciplinary accreditation board
- skill in helping the program convert its courses to an online format
- a high degree of collegiality since rivalries and discord have plagued the department in the past
- a willingness to travel, since out-of-state recruitment and alumni events have become increasingly important to the department
- an international reputation as a scholar, preferably as the recipient of a major award for research
- proficiency in grant writing
- potential to head the department someday
- comfort with asking potential donors for contributions
- good time management skills
- a dynamic classroom presence
- experience in assessment of general education and programs in the department
- a willingness to assume a high service load

The department realizes that this list of desired qualifications and attributes is very long and that some of the items on the list may make others harder to find. The department finds itself at a standstill and has approached you for your advice on how to proceed. What do you recommend?

If you tried to build a position in such a way that only someone qualified to meet all the criteria outlined in this thought experiment could apply, you're likely to have few, if any, applicants. And while our thought experiment may present us with a case that seems excessively, perhaps even ridiculously, specific, it actually isn't all that different from where many departments find themselves when they're thinking about new positions. They want to have it all, and they expect to be able to find a candidate who can meet these expectations.

That goal probably won't be met, but what *will* happen is that the program will deprive itself of the chance of meeting many excellent candidates who could help the department in ways they never thought of. Those candidates will either not apply at all because they'll see that they don't meet the requirements for the position or be screened out by the search committee because they don't meet the established criteria.

When faced with a long list of desired credentials, attributes, areas of experience, or personal traits like the one in our thought experiment, it can be helpful to sort them using a two-step process. First, group the items into three categories: those that are essential, those that are highly desirable, and those that would simply be nice to have.

In our thought experiment, the person or group in charge of defining this position might decide that being able to contribute to the new program in transnational prenuptial agreement studies is essential because this position is part of a strategic hiring plan. Perhaps it would also be decided that essential aspects of the position are the ability to teach the department's proseminar (since the only person qualified to teach it retired a year ago), familiarity with accreditation processes (since no one in the program currently has any experience in this area), and a willingness to assume a high service load (since everyone at the university serves on at least four or five different committees, and people who aren't willing to perform this type of service would never qualify for promotion).

Highly desirable attributes might include gender and ethnic diversity (which approach being an absolute requirement in light of the program's homogeneity but can't actually be required because that would constitute reverse discrimination), skill in helping the program convert its courses to an online format (since that is a major initiative at the university), and proficiency in grant writing. Everything else would simply be nice to have.

The next step in this sorting process is to rank the highly desirable and simply-nice-to-have qualifications in order of priority. If the items in your first category are all truly essential, you should find it impossible to rank those, as, logically, one item cannot be more "absolutely necessary" than another. In fact, if you find that you *can* rank your absolute requirements, you might want to reflect on whether the items that are lower on that list might belong better in the highly desirable category.

As you sort these items, don't try to consider each list in its entirety. Rather, engage in the dual comparison method, which means that you examine only two items at any one time. In our hypothetical example, we said that gender diversity, ethnic diversity, skill in helping the program convert its courses to an online format, and proficiency in grant writing were all highly desirable attributes. Ask yourself, "If I had to choose between two otherwise identical candidates where one brought our program gender diversity and the other brought us ethnic diversity, which would I prefer?"

Suppose, for the sake of continuing our hypothetical example, you decided that ethnic diversity was slightly more important than gender diversity since the faculty already has one woman on it. You would next ask, "If I had to choose between two otherwise identical candidates where one brought our program ethnic diversity and the other brought us skill in helping the program convert its courses to an online format, which would I prefer?" And so on.

By the time you go through the list, you end up with your single most important quality that you regarded as highly desirable. The process then continues as you sort the remaining items in the same way in order to identify the second, third, and fourth most desirable qualities.

Afterward, you rank the simply-nice-to-have items by using the same process. By doing so, you develop a very clear picture of who the sort of person you're hoping to hire should be at the same time that you create a set of screening principles that can be used to help you select semifinalists from among those applicants meeting your basic requirements. Your criteria will be set in such a way that the potential applicants identify the type of person you need while also increasing the likelihood that you'll identify candidates who possess some, though probably not all, of the traits you want.

PUTTING IT ALL TOGETHER

What we've seen in this chapter is that all too many faculty searches start off headed in the wrong direction because the positions themselves were defined in a flawed or inadequate manner. The following are some of the most important principles that deans, chairs, and search committees need to keep in mind when defining faculty positions:

A faculty member is more than just the sum of his or her credentials.

Don't become so preoccupied with credentials and experience that you fail to see each applicant as a whole person. Search committees need to be mindful of the candidate's personal attributes and interpersonal skills because these factors, more than anything else, will make the person a good colleague.

- New or vacant positions give us an opportunity to review our current mix of skills, qualifications, personality traits, and possible contributions and how that mix addresses our needs and desires for the future. Particularly when hiring a replacement for a faculty member who's leaving, it's important to think beyond merely hiring someone to do what the previous person did. Zero-base faculty recruitment enables people to think of the program more holistically, potentially shifting some responsibilities among existing faculty members, rather than assuming that a new member of the group must be able to address every unmet need.
- In order to help programs and institutions refine their identities in an increasingly crowded educational marketplace, strategic hiring provides a mechanism for those involved with searches to think from beyond what currently exists to what may be possible. Properly done, strategic hiring creates synergy among departments and colleges, producing results that are far greater than those that individual programs can achieve on their own.
- Identifying an institution's pillars and platforms of excellence is often the best way to begin developing a strategic hiring plan.
- It's important not to define positions so narrowly that one may inadvertently exclude applicants who would have been even better additions to the program than the candidates who meet the overly specific criteria set in a highly focused search.

Although we've touched briefly in this chapter on the issue of attaining diversity through faculty hiring, that topic is so important—and can affect how we both define positions and search for suitable candidates—that we need to turn next to a more thorough discussion of how to help a program attain its diversity goals when conducting a search.

Chapter 3

Interviewing the Candidates

The most common way for chairs, deans, and other hiring authorities to select which applicant for a faculty position to hire is to conduct an employment interview. Unfortunately, employment interviews are notoriously poor ways of choosing the right candidate. As Ori and Rom Brafman discuss in their book *Sway: The Irresistible Pull of Irrational Behavior* (2008), interviews often cause us to make poor hiring decisions for three reasons.

1. We don't ask the right questions.
2. We ignore objective data.
3. We give too much credence to irrelevant factors. (Brafman and Brafman, 2008, 80–88)

As I've argued in *Best Practices for Faculty Search Committees*, we could avoid most of these problems if we spent less time on *question-and-answer interviewing* and devoted more of our time to *performance-based interviewing* (Buller, 2017, 73–77).

In performance-based interviewing, candidates don't just *tell* you how they'd perform on the job; they *show* you. You watch them teach several different types of courses. You watch them conduct their research. You watch their interactions with others on committees. Some of these opportunities to perform are created on-site when a candidate is brought to your institution for a campus visit. Others occur in the candidate's current work environment and are observed at a distance via Skype or videoconferencing.

Performance-based interviewing gives us a better understanding of how a candidate will actually perform in a real academic environment because the method requires the candidate to make decisions in real time about the types of challenges that occur in a real academic environment. On the other hand,

question-and-answer interviewing is so ingrained in academic search processes and such an established tradition that eliminating it entirely is unlikely.
So, what we need to do is to find better ways of interviewing candidates,
techniques for asking them performance-based questions instead of questions
that aren't very helpful in leading us to the right candidate for the position,
and improved approaches for examining what a candidate tells us during an
interview.

ASKING BETTER QUESTIONS

Let's begin to explore how to ask better interview questions by returning to
the observations of Ori and Rom Brafman in *Sway*. The Brafmans note that
human resource professionals in any corporate setting generally ask variations of ten questions during job interviews.

1. Why should I hire you?
2. What do you see yourself doing five years from now?
3. What do you consider to be your greatest strengths and weaknesses?
4. How would you describe yourself?
5. What college subject did you like the best and the least?
6. What do you know about our company?
7. Why did you decide to seek a job with our company?
8. Why did you leave your last job?
9. What do you want to earn five years from now?
10. What do you really want to do in life? (Brafman and Brafman, 2008,
    80–81)

The Brafmans further note that the only acceptable question among these
ten is the number six: It at least determines the extent to which the applicant
was committed enough to the job at that particular company to do a little
advance research.

All the other questions have severe flaws. Questions one, three, and four
are so obvious that every candidate expects them and knows how to answer
them in ways that an interviewer wants to hear. Questions two, nine, and ten
merely ask the candidate to speculate about the future and once again provide
an obvious answer that the interviewer wants to hear. Questions five, seven,
and eight invite the candidate to reconstruct the past (again in ways that the
interviewer will want to hear). (See Brafman and Brafman, 2008, 81–83.)

None of these standard interview questions—and variations of them are
just as common in academic settings as they are in the corporate world—tell

you what they really want to know: What will this person be like as a colleague with whom I interact day after day, year after year? The key to conducting effective interviews is to remember the following:

> **Interviews should never be about a candidate's qualifications; they should always be about the candidate's fit for your program's greatest needs.**

If you still have questions about a candidate's qualifications when you bring the candidate to campus for an interview, then either you or the search committee didn't do a good enough job reviewing the applications. Cover letters, résumés, and copies of transcripts are enough to tell you who *can* do the job. An interview should tell you whom you *want* to do the job.

In *Facilitating a Collegial Department in Higher Education* (2011), Robert E. Cipriano provides seven questions that were field-tested in faculty interviews at Southern Connecticut State University and found to be most productive in determining a candidate's suitability for a faculty position.

1. What were your most creative contributions to promoting rapport among your colleagues?
2. Every department has its own "dysfunctionality quotient." In your last position, what were the quirks, and how did you deal with them?
3. In what areas do you typically have the least amount of patience in working with your fellow faculty members?
4. If we were to ask your colleagues to describe your strengths and weaknesses in communicating with other faculty members, students, and management, what would they say?
5. Tell us about a conflict you had with a colleague in the past that, looking back, you would have handled differently.
6. All of us have core principles, values, or beliefs that we view as nonnegotiable. What issues would cause you to "go to the mat"?
7. Which of the following three factors would play the most significant role in your decision to accept the offer from this institution: (a) the university; (b) the position you are applying for; (c) the people you would be working with? (Cipriano, 2011, 37–38)

These questions certainly assume that you've already determined that the faculty member has the appropriate credentials and experience to do the job. But simply being able to do the job doesn't mean that the applicant is the best person to do the job. What Cipriano's questions do is cause the candidate to think of specific examples of situations from which you can learn about his or her interpersonal style, approach to conflict, preferred method of communication, and core values. That's a lot more informative than finding out what someone hopes to earn in five years.

For further examples of better questions to ask during an interview, see Buller (2017, 121–124).

FOCUSING ON OBJECTIVE EVIDENCE

When interviewing is truly performance based, it's much easier to focus on objective evidence. Rather than talking about teaching, the candidate actually teaches several classes in several different formats (large, small, online, lab- or studio-based, etc.), and you can draw your own opinions about how effective his or her technique is. Rather than talking about research plans, the candidate provides multiple publications, gives a research-based presentation in whichever format is commonly used at professional conferences in that discipline, and provides a virtual tour (via Skype or videoconferencing) of his or her current research facilities. Rather than talking about service, the candidate sits in on the meetings of several committees, participates in those groups as he or she would if actually a member, and submits a short sample of a committee report or curriculum proposal. In each case, the evidence is right before your eyes, and you gain a good sense of what kind of contribution the person would make to your program.

Because, however, most programs find it too radical to make a complete shift from question-and-answer interviewing to performance-based interviewing, the second-best option is to ask questions about specific aspects of performance rather than general issues of strategy or philosophy. Those specifics can be obtained in two ways: through questions about actual events and through questions about hypothetical situations. Let's begin by examining how to craft questions so that you focus on objective evidence by asking about actual events.

It's easy in the brief period of an interview for candidates to play a role. They want to be on their best behavior and to appear to be the sort of person you'd be eager to hire. Maintaining that façade is much harder if you ask questions that are not general in nature but rather are tied to specific decisions and events. Asking "What is your philosophy of teaching?" is simply a prompt for an applicant to speak in general terms about promoting student engagement and encouraging student success. Asking a candidate for three examples of specific actions he or she has taken to promote student engagement and encourage student success is likely to be much more revealing.

For this reason, it's useful to construct interview prompts that begin with variations of the following:

- Give me three specific examples of when you . . .
- Walk me through your thought process when you . . .
- Talk about several instances when you . . .
- Describe several situations in which you . . .
- What steps did you follow when you . . .

Notice several things about the way in which these prompts are constructed. When asking for examples, they always ask for *multiple* examples. Every candidate comes to an interview with his or her best achievement, biggest failure, and most surprising result in mind. The first answer you'll receive is thus the prepared answer. It's only when you probe for second, third, and fourth examples that you'll get the truly revealing insights.

Second, these prompts don't ask candidates about their philosophy of teaching, research, or service; they ask the candidates to give evidence of that philosophy in action. Certainly once a person is hired and you're mentoring your new faculty member for further success, you'll want to encourage the person to reflect on why he or she has made certain choices and what those choices mean in terms of his or her fundamental approach to being a college professor. In interviews, however, objective evidence is more likely found in specific examples than in vague principles.

Third, a number of the prompts urge the candidate to give you both an example and a rationale. They urge the candidate to speak about his or her thought process or the steps a person took in trying to reach a particular goal. These are the questions that give you insight into the person's philosophy of teaching, research, and action. They give you a chance to see that philosophy in action, not prepackaged so that it will look attractive in an interview (although not really reflective of decisions the person would actually make on the job).

The other way of obtaining objective information is to pose questions based on hypothetical situations. This type of question is almost impossible to prepare for. A good hypothetical situation should be specific enough to be realistic but general enough to allow for several acceptable approaches. If there's only one correct answer to the question, candidates will probably guess the answer you're looking for and deliver it to you regardless of whether they'd truly respond that way if confronted with that situation.

The following is an example of the type of hypothetical situation that works well in an interview.

Imagine that you're at a department meeting where the atmosphere seems tense and highly politicized. Since you're relatively new, you don't understand what the issues are that are causing the conflict, but it's clear that there are several distinct factions and that these individual differences are interfering with the work of the program. Matters can't proceed to a vote because anytime anyone makes or seconds a motion, someone from another faction always objects, and an argument ensues. You're disturbed because the meeting is wasting your time and damaging the program, but you feel vulnerable because you know that others in the room will be voting on your promotion and tenure. What do you decide to do?

There are several courses of action the person could take, and that decision (along with any follow-up questions you may ask) will tell you a great deal about what sort of colleague this person is likely to be. Candidates may reply that they'd sit back and listen until they understand the cause of the conflict better. They may choose to confide in a mentor who can help them work their way through this troubled environment. They may elect to speak out openly even at the risk of their own careers. Whatever their answers are, however, they're probably more indicative of what those candidates would actually do in a difficult situation than their responses to a general question like, "What is your philosophy of conflict resolution?"

IGNORING IRRELEVANT FACTORS

Even the most experienced academic leader can sometimes become distracted by irrelevant factors during a search. One candidate has a credential that seems to us particularly impressive or answers a question in a manner that strikes us as refreshing, and we somehow start to ignore all the other red flags that we would otherwise have noted throughout the search. Or we become convinced that it's absolutely vital for an applicant to have had experience teaching a particular course, and so we overlook the fact that none of the applicants who taught the course taught it particularly well.

In searches, academic leaders sometimes suffer from what we might call *résumé blindness*: the tendency to fixate on credentials and areas of experience that can be documented and thus to neglect intangible, interpersonal factors that contribute significantly to a faculty member's success. Certainly there are many valid reasons for being concerned about credentials and areas of experience. Higher education is in the business of producing credentials; if we didn't care about degrees, we wouldn't spend so much time arguing about the programs that grant them. Moreover, our accrediting bodies required our faculty members to be qualified to teach in their disciplines, and those qualifications depend primarily on credentials and areas of experience.

Nevertheless, the reasons why a faculty member succeeds or fails is only rarely a function of the degrees the person holds or the types of experience he or she has gained. Decisions about promotion and tenure are usually based on the quality of research the person conducts after joining the faculty, so hiring authorities have to try to predict the future: Based on what the person has accomplished so far, is it likely that he or she will produce the level of research needed to succeed in this environment? Based on the effectiveness the person has had so far in teaching, is he or she likely to be effective as a teacher at our institution?

While the answers to those questions are undoubtedly related to the degrees the person holds and the places where the person has studied and worked, we may easily be distracted by a diploma issued by a prestigious institution, a postdoc conducted at a highly selective research center, or a visiting appointment at a well-known institution. Prestige and selectivity may be wonderful things, but we shouldn't let them blind us to the flaws of a candidate who may have peaked early in his or her career, had the good fortune to be in the right place at the right time, or flourished in an environment so different from our own that those experiences really aren't comparable.

In addition, we have to remember the extent to which a faculty member's ability to work with others collegially and professionally determines his or her success after hiring. The likelihood that a faculty member will meet our expectations in this regard can be addressed through the questions by Robert Cipriano that we considered earlier, some well-designed hypothetical situations that each candidate is asked to respond to, and questions posed to the applicant's references. In fact, questions about collegiality and teamwork are among the most important things you can ask during a reference call. Once again, don't merely ask whether the applicant is collegial (every reference will answer yes). Ask instead what the candidate is like when he or she is frustrated, denied support for an idea that he or she thinks is important, or behaving at his or her worst. The more focused your questions are, the more likely you'll receive a reply that is helpful in making the right decision.

ASKING THE RIGHT QUESTIONS

Earlier in this chapter we saw five ways to begin an interview question so that it elicits a performance-based response. The idea is that a good interview question isn't always a question per se. It's often more of a prompt that requires candidates to give you specific examples of decisions they've made or the thought process they used to achieve a particular result. We can now combine any of those introductions with the following phrases to create an interview prompt that tells you what you need to know and allows you to ignore irrelevant factors.

For example, you could follow the introductory prompt "Give me three specific examples of when you . . ." with any of the following:

- were able to help students understand a difficult concept or process.
- discovered a better way of teaching a unit because you initially tried something that didn't work.

- worked with a student outside of class and had some kind of breakthrough.
- were surprised by the degree of your student's progress.
- were proud of an individual student's achievement.
- overcame what initially seemed an insurmountable obstacle in your research.
- were able to secure the funding you needed to support a scholarly endeavor.
- rewrote and successfully resubmitted an article for publication.
- gave valuable assistance to a colleague with his or her own research.
- were excited about a discovery you'd made because it represented an important step forward in your research.
- had an idea or proposal rejected even though you believed in it.
- felt that you were truly acting like a team player.
- disagreed with a colleague in a polite and constructive manner.
- changed your mind about something because the evidence didn't support your initial view.
- were frustrated or annoyed by the behavior of others.
- saw someone doing something and thought, "I could do better than that."
- realized that you were definitely in the right field of scholarly endeavor.
- admired particular qualities in your colleagues.
- disagreed with your supervisor.
- were concerned about the state of higher education.
- worked your way through a crisis.
- ended a day thinking, "Now, *that* was a good day."
- believed that you didn't get the credit you were due.
- accomplished more in a single week than you would have thought possible.
- juggled many different obligations successfully.
- had a valuable experience, though you wouldn't want to repeat it.

If the candidate simply provides the examples that you requested but doesn't tell you why he or she selected them or what was in his or her mind at the time, be sure to ask a follow-up question. Remember that your goal isn't to find out *whether* the applicant can do the job (the person wouldn't have reached the stage of an interview if he or she couldn't), but whether this person is the best fit for your program's current needs and goals.

THE POSITIVE AND NEGATIVE ROLES OF SOCIAL MEDIA

Social media can play a beneficial role during the search process, but it can also have harmful effects on a faculty member's success and ability to make a constructive contribution to the work of a college or university. The beneficial role is easy to summarize: Websites sponsored by publications like *The Chronicle of Higher Education* and various professional organizations make it much easier for an institution to advertise a position quickly and convey its message to a qualified group of potential applicants.

At the same time, the widespread use of social media does pose potential problems for institutions that hire faculty members whose online presence is likely to interfere with the school's ability to fulfill its mission effectively. Certainly, no college or university wants to be in the position of (or even be perceived as) restricting a faculty member's freedom of speech or ability to exchange ideas with others in an unfettered and constructive manner. But institutions of higher education can find their reputations, opportunities to secure external funding, and even their ability to attract students jeopardized by applicants whose social media presence includes postings that celebrate or appear to support excessive drinking, the use of illegal drugs, casual and promiscuous sexual encounters, and any other activity that may commonly be regarded as unbecoming for an academic professional. Moreover, while political speech is the most highly protected of all forms of public exchanges, postings that appear to support acts of terrorism or to represent the institution as a whole rather than the individual writer's opinion can have serious ramifications for both the faculty member and the school.

Public institutions and others that receive any type of federal support (e.g., grants and student scholarship funding) must be careful about asking questions that seem to imply that candidates don't support particular political parties or candidates. The right of candidates to affiliate with political parties is protected no less than their right to affiliate with any other legal organization. Professors at publicly supported institutions have the right to support candidates, parties, and positions of their choice, even if those views run counter to those of senior administrators. A candidate who is asked a question about political affiliation and then does not receive an offer of employment may assume that the decision was made in violation of his or her civil rights and could have grounds for a lawsuit. (See Buller, 2017, 110.)

On the other hand, private institutions, particularly those with a religious affiliation, may have a different obligation and perspective regarding a prospective candidate's controversial statements on social media. And each institution will have to decide for itself what it will regard as permissible personal opinion and inadvisable public expression when considering the social media presence of current and prospective faculty members. In any case, the impact of social media is no longer an issue that hiring authorities can ignore in faculty searches. It's simply good practice to have a plan for what you will ask candidates about in terms of their use of social media and how their responses will enter into your decisions. At some schools, asking an applicant for the ability to review what he or she has posted on Facebook, through Twitter, via Instagram, and so on, will seem indefensibly intrusive and unnecessary. At other schools, that request will be regarded as merely a prudent aspect of your due diligence. Regardless of the perspective your institution takes on these issues, you'll want to be well aware of its position before you begin asking questions of candidates.

USING INTERVIEWS TO SELL YOUR INSTITUTION

One great advantage of basing hiring decisions on performance-based, rather than traditional, interviews, according to Ori and Rom Brafman in *Sway,* is that you can use the time you save from asking a lot of questions that don't reveal very much to do a better job of selling the candidate on the desirability of the job (Brafman and Brafman, 2008, 88). But even in situations where it isn't possible to eliminate standard question-and-answer interviewing from the search process, academic leaders can do a better job of selling their institutions to candidates even before the successful applicant is selected.

Academic leaders sometimes forget that, even when they're interviewing candidates, the candidates are also interviewing them. Just as we want to know whether a particular applicant might be the best fit for us, that candidate also wants to know whether our institution is one where he or she would like to work each day. Is our community one in which the person we're interviewing will want to live and bring his or her family? Are the other faculty members in the program likely to be good colleagues?

If we treat the interview process as though we're doing the candidate a favor by taking time from our busy schedules to talk, we're unlikely to leave a positive impression. It's no longer the case (if it ever was) that by being aloof or adopting a condescending attitude we can make our programs seem like ones from which the applicant would be lucky to receive an offer. By not being welcoming, we're much more likely to alienate candidates than impress them.

A good interview strategy, therefore, is to combine remarks that celebrate the institution, program, and community with performance-based questions relevant to what the person will be doing on the job. Talk about what you and others find most appealing about this environment and ask the candidate how he or she might take advantage of those opportunities. Celebrate the achievements of the faculty members who will be the new person's colleagues. Identify those qualities that make the institution one that students want to attend and where professors choose to spend their careers. If you do a thorough job making the school and community seem attractive now, you'll have an easier time negotiating an offer with a highly desirable candidate later.

PUTTING IT ALL TOGETHER

Interviews are often missed opportunities in higher education. They don't tell the interviewer what he or she really needs to know, waste people's time, and all too often leave a bad impression on the person being interviewed. They run candidates ragged, with meeting after meeting in which they're asked the same questions by different people and are barely given a chance to visit the restroom or have a meal in peace. A good interview should be one in which you have a genuine opportunity to discover whether the candidate is someone you'd want to spend years working with and where the candidate has a genuine opportunity to discover whether the institution is one where he or she would be happy working.

In poor interviews, academic leaders ask questions that the candidates know they'll be asked in advance. The candidates then give answers that they think the interviewer wants to hear, even though those answers may not be the most honest or revealing. To whatever extent possible, a good interview should be performance based: You should have a realistic opportunity to see the candidate performing the tasks that he or she would actually have to do if hired. But because a switch from traditional question-and-answer interviewing to a purely performance-based approach seems too revolutionary for most colleges and universities, academic leaders can at least phrase their questions in a way that requires the candidate to provide specific examples of what he or she has done and specific reasons for doing so. The best way to achieve this goal is to replace as many questions as possible with performance-based prompts that require concrete examples and a candid reflection on why the applicant chose the course of action described in the example.

Chapter 4

Making the Decision

Once the search committee has held interviews, contacted references, and asked stakeholders about their impressions of each candidate, it's time to make a decision about whom to hire. But in order to make that decision effectively, everyone involved in the process needs to know who is actually making that decision and what his or her own role is in the process. More than one search committee has been bitterly disappointed because it believed that it was choosing which candidate to hire when, in fact, the chair, dean, or provost was to select the successful candidate.

Best practices suggest that this information should have been shared with the search committee at its very first meeting, but those who are running the meeting sometimes forget. Search committee members forget things as well, and even if they were initially told that they wouldn't have the final word in the hiring decision, they may not recall that discussion by the time the interviews conclude.

In most cases, a search committee is not regarded by the institution as a decision-making body but as a fact-finding and advisory body that performs a service for the school's administration or governing board. That distinction provides an extra layer of legal protection if a disgruntled candidate sues the institution for unfair labor practices. It will then be the individual or group with full hiring authority who has to answer the complaint, not the members of the search committee themselves.

Because of the possibility for misunderstandings to arise during this crucial decision-making stage, it's useful for the search chair to begin the discussions about the finalists and the results of the interviews by reiterating the answers to the following questions:

- Who will be making the final decision?
- Who will be making recommendations that guide the final decision?
- In what form will those recommendations be made?

The last of these questions is of particular importance since institutional policy or the academic leader's own preferences may shape how the search committee and others deliver their recommendations. The number of ways in which a hiring recommendation can be made is almost equal to the number of administrators who receive these recommendations, but the following are the most common:

- a single name and justification, essentially answering the question, "If the choice were yours to make, whom would you hire and why?"
- a list that divides the finalists into acceptable and unacceptable choices
- a priority ranking of the finalists, perhaps also divided into acceptable and unacceptable choices
- an unranked list of preferred choices
- a list of pros and cons for each finalist
- individual recommendations from each member of the search committee

In this chapter, we'll also consider one slight variant of these methods that some academic leaders may find more useful than these other traditional formats. But before we do that, we need to explore how the search committee will go about making its selection, regardless of the form that the recommendation takes.

GATHERING INFORMATION

Although you, as the hiring agent, will want to rely on your own impressions when choosing the person who will receive the offer—and justifiably so since making this decision is your responsibility—you also need to consider the advice of other stakeholder groups. As you think about the best way to gather this information, keep in mind the following best practices in faculty hiring:

- On any type of response form or online survey that you develop, participants should be asked to identify whether they're on the search committee, in the department that is hiring the faculty member, or otherwise associated with the institution. There may be cases where the opinions of certain stakeholder groups matter more in developing the recommendation than those of other groups. For example, if many faculty members in a candidate's potential department say they feel they can't work with him or her, that result may matter more than the responses of 95% of all other constituencies that express no reservation.

- Participants should be asked to specify the basis on which they are making their recommendation, as this information is useful in case certain discrepancies appear. For example, people who only review the candidate's written materials may be favorably impressed, while those who meet the candidate in person may have a more negative impression. If you don't know what the person completing the form has reviewed, it may be impossible to make sense of a highly bimodal set of responses.
- It's helpful for respondents to report the actual meetings and appointments they participated in during each candidate's visit. For example, rather than asking people whether they attended "a small meeting or Q+A session," it may be desirable to ask whether they attended the "9:00 a.m. open session for staff" or the "1:00 p.m. meet and greet with division heads." Rather than asking individuals whether they attended a sample class, it may be useful to ask them to specify *which* sample class they attended, if several were offered.
- People shouldn't be asked to comment just on the finalist's teaching, research, and service, as these qualities are addressed on many candidate evaluation forms, but also on such issues as the individual's interpersonal skills, fit, ability to enhance diversity, and potential for the future. In many cases, those are the issues that search committees end up discussing at length in their deliberations, even though stakeholders weren't asked to comment on those aspects of the applicant's interview. By having these items on the evaluation form, stakeholders are reminded that it isn't academic qualifications alone that determine whether a candidate will succeed if hired, and, in addition, the search committee will have more impressions than merely their own from which to draw conclusions.
- People should be asked to identify each candidate's strengths and weaknesses because, as we'll discuss in a moment, consideration of strengths and weaknesses is a valuable component of a search committee's deliberations. Those who interact with candidates, however, often aren't asked to describe them, and, as a result, the search committee members may simply rely on their own experiences (which could be different from those of others) or, worse, misunderstand a comment made by an interviewer. For example, someone might write, "The candidate has very strong opinions about how the curriculum should be improved," viewing this decisiveness as an asset, while the search committee may interpret the remark as a criticism of the candidate's stubbornness and unwillingness to accept ideas different from his or her own.

- People should be asked not only whether they recommend that the candidate be hired but also about the *strength* of that recommendation (strongly recommend, recommend, recommend with reservations, or not recommend), as that information helps the committee rank the candidates, if a ranking is requested of them. There can be a great deal of difference in the strength of a recommendation: It can range anywhere from "This candidate seems acceptable if no one else can be found" to "Hire this candidate!" By asking the person completing the form to specify the degree to which he or she is recommending each candidate, the committee can develop a more nuanced portrait of how various stakeholder groups feel.
- It is often helpful to collect stakeholder impressions in electronic form rather than via hard-copy surveys because online forms process information in a way that's easier to tabulate than what can be gathered from paper forms. Certain questions can be required and do not allow the person to continue without answering them. Data will be more consistent because users can be guided to select specific items from a menu rather than answering each question freeform in a manner that might complicate comparisons among candidates.
- Rather than using a generic response form, it's a good idea to develop one of your own that emphasizes the specific focus of the position. For example, if you're working at a community college, you may want one or two questions about the candidate's research while focusing a lot more intently on his or her teaching and service. Conversely, a research university may wish to increase the emphasis placed on research, while reducing the emphasis placed on service (and possibly teaching as well).

Regardless of how the evaluation form is adapted, the guiding principle should be the following:

A well-designed candidate evaluation form should focus on those items that will most help the committee to make its decision. At the same time, the form should be as easy as possible for reviewers to complete it since overly complex forms tend to be ignored.

When processing the information gained from the people who interacted with the candidate, don't just count up positive and negative responses. The evaluation forms aren't ballots, and people aren't electing a candidate.

When we vote in an election, every vote counts equally, but that may not be the case when a search committee reviews evaluation forms. An observation like "This person's research seems trivial and uninspired" carries far more weight if it is said by the department chair than if it is said by an undergraduate. And, as we saw before, search committees often pay far more attention to the views of those in the department where the faculty member will be working than those whose teaching and research won't be much affected by the new hire.

The key questions when reviewing information supplied by evaluation forms are the following:

1. **What does the respondent say?**
2. **Who is the respondent?**
3. **On what basis is the respondent making his or her judgment?**

ACHIEVING CONSENSUS

If you chair the search committee as it begins discussing which candidate to recommend, it's best to have the group discuss each candidate individually rather than immediately focusing on which candidate various members of the committee prefer. If you turn at once to who seems to be the best candidate, people with stronger or more forceful views may cause others on the committee to remain silent, even if they favor other candidates. By going through all the finalists individually and asking members to summarize the strengths and weaknesses of each, you're more likely to receive a complete picture of what the candidates could bring to the position if they were offered the job.

It's probably a good idea to discuss the candidates in the order they were interviewed. The first candidate is sometimes at a disadvantage because memories of what later candidates said are fresher and also because the interviewing skills of the committee can improve over time: They may not have thought to ask the first candidate about an issue that arose only in subsequent interviews and unconsciously downgrade that person's status because he or she never had a chance to address that issue. By proceeding systematically through the finalists, therefore, you help prevent the committee from rushing to judgment and ultimately reach a better decision.

If following this discussion there appears to be a candidate who clearly has almost everyone's support, it may be possible to complete this stage of the process either by a vote or by simply asking, "Are we all in agreement then?" (Once again, you don't want to rely on that kind of oral procedure anytime you feel that peer pressure may be compelling certain members of the committee to defer to others.)

When views appear to be less homogeneous, however, you'll need to probe a little further: Which candidates do various members consider completely unacceptable and why? When individual members of the search committee say that they support a given candidate, how strong is that support?

In other words, how would they rate the candidate on a scale from 1 (minimally acceptable) to 10 (an obvious superstar)? Can the members of the search committee articulate the reasons why other members prefer different candidates? Which of those reasons seems most compelling?

In the end, it's always better for the search committee to send a consensus recommendation than a simple majority vote forward to the next level. With searches that leave the committee highly divided, the person who receives the recommendation may best be served by getting two different reports: one from the majority and one from the minority. In this way, his or her own recommendation or decision will be better informed than if the report includes only the perspectives of the side whose favored candidate received the most votes.

In addition, if a vote is taken, it's valuable for the hiring authority to know the vote count on each side: A seven-to-six majority may be interpreted quite differently from a twelve-to-one majority. In fact, in cases where only one or two committee members vote differently from the rest of the committee, it's advisable to ask if a second vote can be taken to see if unanimity is possible. That type of strong consensus will often carry far more weight with deans and provosts than even the most lopsided vote if there's still disagreement among members of the committee.

Questions to reflect on when deciding which finalist to recommend for the position:

1. What do I most want to happen after this position is filled?
2. What do I want *never* to happen?
3. What sort of situations will this person encounter?
4. What sort of people will this person encounter?
5. If we hire this person, how could he or she provide us with something important we don't already have?
6. How might this person harmonize with the people and programs we do already have?
7. Where have I made mistakes in hiring before? How can I do better this time?
8. What are my own preconceptions to watch out for? (e.g., Ivy League graduates are "always better" than public university graduates.)

DECISIONS AT OTHER LEVELS

As we saw earlier, search committees almost never actually make hiring decisions, as those decisions are usually made by whichever level of the institution is designated as the official hiring authority. (As I mentioned in the Introduction, I'm assuming for the purposes of this book that's you or that you at least play a substantive role in making that decision.) At most colleges and universities, deans or department chairs serve as the hiring authority.

Nevertheless, depending on the school's policies or bylaws, that responsibility could be assigned to any level from the chair of the search committee to the governing board. For this reason, when a search committee is making its recommendation, the important questions for it to consider are the following:

- At what level will the final hiring decision be made?
- How many levels of recommendation are there between the search committee and the hiring authority?
- What does the hiring authority and each level of recommendation in between need to know in order to make an informed decision?

In most cases, the format that the committee's recommendation will take to the next level is spelled out in either existing policies or the committee's initial charge.

We've seen that common forms for recommendations to take include the name of a single candidate, a ranked list of candidates, an unranked list of acceptable candidates, pros and cons of each candidate, and so on. While the format of a recommendation may be specified, however, a committee may also decide that it wants to provide some informal background for that recommendation. For example, even if asked to make a formal recommendation that consists of an unranked list of acceptable finalists, the search chair may wish to add an informal oral summary of the committee's preference for one or more candidates.

Similarly, if there are still several administrative levels separating the search committee from the hiring authority, it may be desirable to provide some context that will help others in developing their recommendations and decisions. For example, suppose that a search committee is making a recommendation to a department chair, who then passes on a recommendation to a dean, who in turn makes a recommendation to the provost, who makes the final decision on whom to hire.

The search committee may be aware of retirement plans of one or more members of the faculty, recently emerging developments within the discipline, likely enrollment trends for various tracks within the program, or other matters that shaped their recommendation. A summary of these issues will help subsequent administrative levels understand not merely what the recommendation is but also why it is being made, and it can assist those who have to make recommendations or decisions about programs with which they may have only occasional involvement. The background information makes it clear that the decision committee members weren't simply recommending a person with whom they felt the greatest rapport but rather recommending the person who best fit the larger needs of the department, college or division, and institution.

DEALING WITH DISSENT FROM HIGHER LEVELS

Since search committees are only making recommendations that can be accepted or rejected at higher administrative levels, it sometimes happens that a dean or provost will extend an offer to a candidate whom the search committee didn't support. That outcome may occur for several different reasons:

- The administrator may feel that the program needs to move in a new or different direction and believe that the committee's recommendation doesn't reflect that need for change.
- The administrator may be concerned with different aspects of the position from those given priority by the search committee. For example, the search committee may have emphasized excellence in teaching while the dean was more concerned about grant activity.
- The administrator may believe that a candidate who brings diversity to the program should have been given more consideration.
- The administrator may have the impression that the search committee did not adequately follow established procedures, rushed to judgment, or otherwise failed to live up to its responsibilities.

It's never pleasant, of course, to have your advice ignored or your recommendation overturned, but no one should expect his or her boss to agree with every recommendation. The key questions for the search committee to ask at this point would be, what kind of decision is this? Is it one we can live with, one that we should caution against, or one that we should actively dispute as likely to be destructive to our program?

If the decision is one that you can live with, you're probably better off accepting it and working as constructively as possible to make that faculty member successful. While it's a common faculty practice to try to resist any decision that goes against their desires, that practice can be counterproductive in the long run.

Administrators react to disagreement much like anyone else: They accommodate opposing views when they can, but there are limits to how much flexibility they can or are willing to provide. Think of it this way: Imagine that each of us has only a certain number of "chits" that we can use to "purchase" reversal of a decision once it's been made. If you use all your "chits" on relatively insignificant matters, you won't have enough left for the truly important matters.

More specifically, faculty members who regularly oppose decisions that administrators are fully authorized to make run the risk of getting dismissed as whiners or knee-jerk opponents of any administrative action whatsoever. If the hiring decision is one that you yourself wouldn't have made but that you can tolerate (or maybe even come to accept), you're better off simply going along with it and concluding that you just can't win them all.

If, however, you conclude that the decision being made by the hiring authority would cause genuine harm to the program, then you have an obligation to raise these concerns before a final commitment is made to the candidate. In expressing these concerns, it's important to keep several considerations in mind:

- Identify as specifically as possible the harm that you believe will be caused by this hire. If objections are too vague—something along the lines of, "We just don't think this candidate is a good fit for us," or "We have some concerns about whether this finalist's research will progress sufficiently for a favorable tenure review in six years"—they're likely to be dismissed as out of hand. Ask yourself what negative impact the candidate will have on your program and why the hiring authority should be concerned.
- Document the evidence that has caused you to reach this conclusion. If it was a comment that the candidate made during the interview, quote it as precisely as you can, and compare your recollections with any other witnesses who heard it. If it was something that appeared in the candidate's application documents, include a copy of that document with your statement of concern and clearly mark the passage in question. Remember that the person to whom you're addressing your concerns will want to focus on specific evidence, not mere impressions, perceptions, or assumptions.
- Try to look at the issue from the perspective of the hiring authority, as he or she may have priorities that are different from those that faculty members or the department chair in the program may have. If the objection to a candidate is that the program's preferred candidate will lighten the workload of those in the area more than the preferred candidate of the dean or provost, the administrator may not regard that as a compelling enough reason to overturn the decision. It would be far more effective to express your apprehensions in terms that relate to the hiring authority's more important concerns such as if the candidate is likely (for some documentable reason) to cause student retention to decrease, grant funding to suffer, applications to diminish, or the budget to become further constrained.

Keep in mind, too, that no matter how convincing you regard your argument, the hiring authority may always decide to uphold his or her original decision anyway. Administrators do make mistakes, and so, for that matter, do search committees.

While we've been trying throughout this book to identify an exemplary set of best practices in faculty recruitment and hiring, no process will ever become perfect. There will always be times when we have to endure the faulty hiring choices that have been made and try to fix them later. (For a case study exercise on a serious disagreement between a search committee and the dean, see Buller and Cipriano 2015b, 9–10.)

Common mistakes made when hiring faculty members:

- **rushing to make the decision**
- **settling just to fill the position**
- **hiring on intuition**
- **not using any "gut" feelings at all (reason and emotion need to be balanced)**
- **the "halo effect" (a phenomenon that occurs when one very strong aspect overshadows many other positive or negative aspects)**

PUTTING IT ALL TOGETHER

Developing a decision or recommendation on whom to hire as part of a faculty search process isn't as easy as counting the number of favorable "votes" each finalist receives, but a faculty search isn't a popularity contest. Search committees, department chairs, deans, and provosts must all examine the contributions that each candidate could make, align those with the needs of the program and institution as a whole, and then weigh those positive aspects against any deficits the candidate may have.

Everyone involved in the process will want to consider the following questions: Is increasing research productivity important enough that the program could endure hiring a faculty member whose record of collegiality has been less than spectacular? Does a phenomenal record of teaching success compensate for a reluctance to serve on committees? Can an international reputation for publication bring benefits that are more important than evidence of uninspired teaching?

Very few candidates come to us as "the whole package" with no weaknesses whatsoever, and even those who seem perfect when we make them an offer frequently turn out to have a surprising number of flaws once they've been on the job for a year or two. Making a hiring decision, therefore, requires a capacity to look at evidence critically and objectively as well as the abilities to distinguish what is genuine about a candidate as opposed to what may have been an act for the sake of the interview, assess how well a candidate will fit the program and institution right now, and predict what a candidate's potential is for development in the future.

The practices outlined in this chapter will help increase the odds of making the right decision more frequently, but no one gets it right all the time. That's why colleges and universities have other procedures in place, such as annual evaluations, promotion processes, and post-tenure review.

Chapter 5

Closing the Deal

As a hiring authority or someone who works at an administrative level between the search committee and hiring authority, you are likely also to have responsibilities at the next stage in the search process: negotiating an offer with the recommended finalist and closing the deal. Like every other phase of the search process, closing the deal is a more complicated matter than many people imagine.

It's not, as some believe, as straightforward as contacting the chosen candidate, making an offer at a preestablished salary, and receiving a statement of acceptance. Even in an economy where there are many more candidates for positions than there are positions available, closing the deal can involve a surprisingly complicated, serpentine series of negotiations.

Moreover, it's important to remember one of the results that emerged from ATLAS's survey in chapter 1: It is this stage of the recruitment and hiring process that faculty members are least satisfied with. They believe that their efforts in selecting candidates and finalists are often wasted when administrators ignore their recommendations or don't pursue their chosen candidates with sufficient intensity. So, there's a good deal of room for improvement when it comes to how administrators close the deal with their chosen candidates.

The most important thing to remember when preparing to make an offer is the following: *The power dynamic between the two of you is about to change dramatically*. Until now, power was really all on your side: You had something candidates wanted (a job), and they were in a position that required them to impress you. Now they have something you want (acceptance of the position and completion of the search), and you're in a position that requires you to impress them.

Some academic administrators will dispute this observation. "I still hold all the cards," they'll say. "It's take it or leave it. If a candidate starts getting too demanding, I'll just move on to the next one. There are plenty of people who would accept this job in a heartbeat."

To some extent, that situation may be true. There may indeed be plenty of viable, highly qualified candidates still in the pool. But it is more often the case that only one or two finalists rise to the very top in terms of not just qualifications and experience but also those other intangible factors such as "fit" and potential value-added contributions.

You'll have invested a great deal of time and money identifying these candidates, and you won't want them to turn down an offer to join your institution. Besides, even if "there are plenty more fish in the sea," which would you rather have: a finalist who's eager and excited to join you because he or she knows that you're enthusiastic about his or her candidacy, or a finalist who accepts the offer because he or she knows that, unless acceptance comes quickly, you'll move on to a third, fourth, or fifth choice almost immediately?

When preparing to make an offer to a candidate, there are several best practices to keep in mind:

1. **Contact your first choice quickly.**
2. **Know the terms of your offer and the range of your flexibility in advance.**
3. **Be sure the candidate understands how much time he or she has to make a decision.**
4. **Design Plan B in case the candidate rejects the offer. Have your Plan B in mind even before proceeding to Plan A.**

Let's take a brief look at what's involved in each of these practices.

CONTACTING YOUR FIRST CHOICE QUICKLY

A good rule of thumb to keep in mind when preparing to make an offer is that if you're interested in a particular candidate, other programs probably are as well. Even in a market glutted with applicants, the best people often receive multiple offers.

Delaying in making contact carries several disadvantages: First, it gives the candidate additional time to apply for other positions, go on other interviews, and entertain other offers. Second, the lag time allows any excitement the candidate may have developed for the institution during the interview process to diminish. Third, too much lag time can make it seem as though you're not really very interested in him or her; candidates will assume that you may be negotiating with a different applicant; and, if you eventually make an offer, they may assume (rightly or wrongly) that they weren't your first choice.

Job offers are most effective when they're made as soon as possible after the interview has finished. There have been cases in which a successful candidate is contacted by the hiring authority while he or she is still at the airport waiting to fly home or first thing the next morning. That situation requires, of course, that the job is being offered to the last candidate interviewed, which is often not the case, and that the search committee and all subsequent levels of recommendation or approval can come to agreement quickly, which often doesn't occur.

For this reason, the exit meeting with each candidate interviewed should include a realistic assessment of when the decision is likely to be made and the probable time frame for notifying all of the candidates. If that doesn't occur, an occasional quick e-mail update about where the process stands and the likely timetable as it moves forward can go a long way toward keeping your most promising candidates still engaged in the search.

KNOWING THE TERMS OF YOUR OFFER

When most people think about the terms of a job offer, they think largely (and sometimes exclusively) about salary terms. As we'll see in a moment, there are many other factors that can form parts of contract terms, but since salary plays such an overarching role, let's start with it.

Making a salary offer is more complicated than simply knowing what the approved range for the position is and selecting an amount that falls within that range. The other factors that need to be considered are the following:

- the current salaries of others in comparable positions at your institution
- the current salaries of others in comparable positions elsewhere
- the degree of salary compression or inversion that is present among employees
- the degree of flexibility you have in negotiating the salary
- whether other levels of the institution have to approve your recommendations before they can be presented as a formal offer

Salary compression occurs when newly hired employees receive earnings at or near the level of more experienced current employees. For example, suppose you hired an entry-level assistant professor a number of years ago at a salary of $48,000, and this faculty member now holds the rank of full professor and earns $85,000. If this year you hire an associate professor at $83,000, you'll create a case of salary compression.

Salary inversion occurs when new employees are brought in at a rate even higher than that of more experienced employees. In the same hypothetical scenario, if you hire a new associate professor at a rate of $88,000, you'll create a case of salary inversion.

Salary compression and inversion become significant to academic leaders when they have an impact on faculty morale. Even at institutions where salaries are kept confidential, how much people make tends to be a rather open secret, and knowing that someone with less experience makes nearly the same or even more money than you do can change your feelings regarding the new employee from enthusiasm to resentment when six months to a year later it turns out that he or she does not actually walk on water. The question that a hiring authority needs to ask is, "does long-term improvement of salaries in this area or short-term detriment to faculty morale matter more in this case?"

That question is actually more complex than it may appear initially. The answer will depend on whether the person does—or even *can*—take a long-term view of salary matters.

If you're a provost, dean, or chair whose position is open-ended, then it is probably in everyone's best interests to endure a degree of short-term unhappiness about salaries in order to make improvements in the long run. The higher salary helps the new employee immediately, and the inequity resulting from salary compression or inversion can help you make the case for providing additional raises to other employees in the future.

But not everyone is in a position to take this type of long-term view. At some institutions, the position of chair rotates, and a new faculty member heads the department every three to five years, while, at others, the administrator may know that he or she is likely to remain in that position for only one or two more years. No one knows whether the next person will want to continue a policy of hiring in new faculty members at the highest possible level and then trying to adjust the salaries of continuing faculty members accordingly.

The result could be great disparities among the salaries of some faculty members who could then cause severe, intractable morale issues for everyone else. The issues to keep in mind, therefore, are how long a plan that raises salaries in the unit overall by hiring people at the top of the range is likely to remain in place and how significant a problem any resulting morale issues are likely to produce.

Once the hiring authority has given thought to these considerations (a process that can, in fact, be concluded long before the point of making an offer is reached), a decision has to be made about whether to offer the highest salary available or start with a lower offer and allow the candidate to negotiate for a larger amount. Here, again, there are several philosophies to consider.

On one side of the issue, people will suggest that an institution should never put its highest offer on the table immediately since a candidate will always try to negotiate. If you have no room to negotiate, these discussions could either fail or cause the candidate to accept the offer only grudgingly and reluctantly.

On the other side of the issue, people will suggest that hiring a faculty member shouldn't be negotiated as though one were trying to sell a used car, with each side trying to take advantage of the other. If the candidate accepts an amount less than what the institution can offer (and possibly does offer candidates in other comparable searches), the morale problems that result could make the small amount that was saved seem trivial by comparison.

One factor to keep in mind is the range you'd have available for negotiating. If your degree of flexibility is only a few thousand dollars, it's probably not worth holding that amount back from your initial offer.

When candidates make counteroffers, they're almost never only slightly higher than what the institution initially proposes. Candidates will often propose a salary ten, twenty, or thirty thousand dollars higher than the initial offer and, if that occurs, then any effort to increase the salary by a couple thousand dollars will seem paltry. For high-end positions, such as a researcher bringing in multiple millions of dollars' worth of grants or a distinguished senior professor, it may be possible to negotiate a salary with the degree of flexibility needed to meet the candidate's expectations.

If not, the question really becomes, "How badly do you want to recruit this person?" If the answer is, "Not that badly. We have a number of other viable candidates, any of whom would be equally as good," you'll probably want to propose a reasonable and fair salary in light of your budgetary possibilities and negotiate very little from that original position.

If the answer is, "This is the one candidate whom we really want to hire," your approach should be different. One useful strategy is to tell the candidate something like the following: "You're our chosen candidate, and we are serious about wanting you to join our team. As a result, the salary I'm going to offer you is at the very top of our range. I'm not going to have any flexibility to negotiate anything higher than what I propose. We may be able to assist you in other ways, but I need you to understand that the salary I'm going to propose is the absolute best we can do."

When the candidate then asks (as he or she inevitably will) what those "other ways" are in which you might be able to help, it's time to focus on the other elements of the job offer that go beyond salary. Here are a few of the most common additional areas of compensation that arise during the process of closing the deal:

- teaching load
- flexibility in course scheduling
- tenure status (credit for prior service or tenure upon hiring)
- office space
- research space
- access to equipment
- intra-institutional research funding
- grant application assistance
- research assistants
- teaching assistants
- clerical/administrative support
- travel funding
- discretionary funding
- summer salary
- moving expenses
- spousal employment
- child care
- tuition remission for dependents

Your ability to negotiate with candidates about some of these areas of compensation may be restricted by institutional policy or even state law. For example, in some state university systems, it's not possible to grant a faculty member tenure upon hiring, no matter how distinguished his or her record may be, whereas other systems have policies governing the maximum size of faculty offices or the conditions under which moving expenses may be reimbursed. Before you make a formal offer, it's important to know any limitations that may affect what you're able to offer so that you don't find yourself in the embarrassing position of having to renege on a promise made to a candidate.

Although it's never appropriate to ask candidates about their family status or residential living arrangements, that doesn't mean that you have to wait until after an offer is accepted to broach the subject of any family-friendly policies your institution may have. In fact, as long as you provide the same information to every applicant or finalist, you don't even have to wait until the offer stage to make this information available.

It can be quite beneficial to provide information about spousal hiring or placement policies, who is covered by such policies, daycare services, and any other benefits the institution offers its employees earlier in the process or as a recruitment tool. This type of information can help make a candidate accept an offer; it may even induce potential applicants to apply for a position they wouldn't otherwise believe to be right for them.

It's important when providing this information to be absolutely clear about what assistance is provided and whether there are time restrictions or other limitations to the type of assistance available. Help in finding a position is very different from guaranteeing someone a job, and offering to employ a spouse is different from offering to employ an unmarried significant other.

According to ATLAS's survey that was discussed in chapter 1, spousal employment assistance is becoming increasingly common, but it's still far from universal.

- Roughly a quarter of respondents (26.1%) noted that their institutions made no effort at all to find employment for trailing spouses or significant others.
- 41.6% reported that employment assistance did occur, but only rarely.
- About another quarter (24.6%) reported that their schools didn't have formal spousal placement policies but offered employment to faculty members' spouses, partners, or significant others under extraordinary circumstances.
- The remaining 7.7% said that their institutions didn't have a formal policy of spousal placement but did regularly offer assistance or employment if it was requested during contract negotiations.

In most cases, you're entitled to rescind an offer you've made before it is officially agreed to by all parties. For that reason, if a finalist makes a counteroffer that strikes you as excessively demanding or unreasonable, you can revoke your original offer and proceed immediately to your next candidate. (Be sure to check with your institution's legal counsel before doing so, however, since there may be restrictions on your ability to take this action in your state or university system.)

But that option isn't one to take lightly. Candidates usually understand that their best opportunity to secure a compensation package that is to their advantage occurs during the original negotiation of a job offer. For that reason, you shouldn't take it personally when candidates try to do as well for themselves as they can and rescind an offer only when the way in which a candidate tries to negotiate reveals that he or she isn't the sort of person you'd want on your faculty anyway.

SETTING A TIME LIMIT

Another area in which time limits come into play has to do with when the successful finalist needs to notify you about whether he or she will accept the offer. Although candidates do sometimes accept an offer immediately after it's made, this occurrence is rare. More frequently, a candidate will need some time to consider the offer, discuss it with his or her family, examine other options, see a counteroffer from his or her current employer, or gain some broader perspective before making such an important decision.

While you'll certainly want to honor a request to "think it over" (greater buy-in to the institution can result when candidates understand that their legitimate needs are being taken seriously), it's not a good idea to leave this decision open-ended. For one thing, if the candidate doesn't accept your offer, you may want to proceed to other candidates who may be getting recruited by other schools. (See the discussion of your Plan B.) For another thing, a candidate who's keeping your offer as a backup in case nothing better comes along is unlikely to be a faculty member with a strong commitment to the institution anyway.

A time frame of ten days to two weeks to accept an offer is typical. For highly distinguished candidates for whom there are no alternatives, you may want to expand these limits a bit. Late in the recruitment cycle when you need to hire right away, you may want to condense them.

In any case, your written and oral versions of the offer should include a specific time and date after which it becomes invalid. It's much easier to extend a time limit if you need to than to move up a deadline if a candidate seems to be dragging the process out too long.

Moreover, if you decide to amend an offer by increasing the compensation package or altering the starting date, for instance, it's usually best to retain the original deadline for accepting the offer rather than starting a new ten-day or two-week period. If the contract deadline keeps rolling as counteroffers are made and considered, the entire process can easily become so delayed that other viable candidates are no longer available.

KNOWING PLAN B

Having a clear sense of whether there are in fact other viable candidates still in the pool is an important part of developing a Plan B when you make an offer. Your Plan B might include making an offer to another viable candidate, returning to existing pool and adding more candidates to a revised short list, extending the deadline for the position and accepting more applications, reopening the search and developing an entirely new pool of applicants, closing the search and waiting until next year, hiring a candidate in a temporary or part-time capacity, and so on.

Knowing what your Plan B will be when you're still pursuing Plan A helps you in a number of ways: If you're not entirely convinced that a particular candidate is absolutely the best fit for your program, you may decide to be less flexible in negotiating by knowing that you have an adequate backup plan. If a candidate turns down your offer late in the process (or, worse, reneges on an offer that he or she has already accepted), you'll already have thought through how you might still meet your staffing needs. If other viable finalists contact you about the status of the search after an offer has been made but before it's been accepted, you'll have a more realistic sense of what your time frame will be as you move forward.

Regardless of what your Plan B is, however, the important thing will be to implement it as soon as it becomes necessary. Other candidates, either in your current pool or who might apply in a reopened search, will also be looking for other positions. The longer your search process takes, the fewer of these highly attractive candidates will still be available.

Even if you decide to cancel the search and proceed with a temporary or part-time hire, most institutions require at least some lead time in wrapping up one search process before you can begin another. All of these contingencies take time, and precious time can be saved if you know in advance what your Plan B (and perhaps Plans C and D as well) will be even while you're still trying to implement Plan A.

SPECIAL CONSIDERATIONS WHEN HIRING INTERNATIONAL CANDIDATES

Closing the deal becomes a bit more complicated when an international candidate is recommended for the position.

Whenever an institution is considering extending an offer to someone who is not either a citizen or a permanent resident, it is important to consult with an attorney who has expertise in immigration issues and the hiring of noncitizens.

This best practice can't be overemphasized. The rules governing the hiring of employees who are not citizens or permanent residents change frequently, and although every effort has been made to ensure that the advice given here is accurate at the date of publication, subsequent laws may have changed some of the requirements.

In addition, the following information applies only to candidates who aren't citizens or permanent residents of the United States. Other countries have their own laws and requirements and, if you're hiring someone for an institution that's not governed by U.S. law, you'll want to make sure you're acting in accordance with whatever rules do apply to your own situation.

Although you can't ask a candidate for a position about his or her national origin, you can, and indeed *should,* ask whether he or she is legally authorized to work in this country. That's because your institution isn't allowed to hire anyone who isn't so authorized, such as a foreign national who is here on a student or tourist visa, without taking additional steps at the federal level. Foreign nationals who have permanent residency status may receive a job offer and be hired just as a citizen would be.

Holding visas, however, fall into what initially may seem to be a bewildering array of categories, each of which is designated by a different letter of the alphabet. The most common visa categories you may encounter are H, or temporary worker, visas and J visas that designate exchange visitors in programs designated by the Bureau of Consular Affairs of the Department of State.

In most cases, the visa involved will be an H-1B visa, which allows foreign workers to be employed in specialty areas that require expert knowledge in that field. As such, H-1B holders typically possess at least a baccalaureate degree as well as first professional degrees, like the JD or Pharm.D., or terminal degrees for most faculty positions. Moreover, their degree must be in the area of study for which they are being hired.

H-1B visas are valid for three years and can be extended to a maximum of six years. After that time, the visa holder must either have attained or, under certain restrictions, be sufficiently far along in the process of pursuing permanent residency status or remain outside the United States for at least one year before reapplying for an H-1B visa. H-1B visas have limited portability; workers may be permitted to change employers if the new employer petitions the U.S. Citizenship and Immigration Services. Workers holding an H-1B visa are attached to a single employer; they can't be paid additional income by any source other than their primary employer.

In addition, workers with an H-1B visa must be paid the higher of the two following wages: the actual wage (what you would pay to a U.S. citizen with comparable credentials and experience in that field) or the prevailing wage (the amount that the Department of Labor determines to be average for all employees with comparable credentials and experience in that region). Prevailing wage determinations take several months to process, so these applications should be submitted to the government at the earliest possible opportunity. In some cases, the employee may be allowed to start work before the prevailing wage determination is complete, but he or she will have to be paid back wages if the Department of Labor determines that the required wage is higher than what the institution is currently paying.

> **If you are planning to employ the holder of an H-1B visa for more than six years, initiate the process of seeking permanent residency status as soon as possible after the person has been hired.**

In most cases, the J visa involved will be a J-1 visa, which allows research scholars, college faculty members, and exchange visitors to participate in programs that promote cultural exchange or provide training in fields such as medicine or business. Holders of a J-1 visa may usually work only for their program sponsors, so if someone with a J-1 visa sponsored by another institution applies for a job at your school, a new visa will need to be approved before you can legally hire that person.

Certain J-1 visas have a home-residence requirement. If an applicant holds one of these J-1 visas, he or she cannot be converted to an H-1B visa without either a two-year residence in his or her home country or a waiver of this requirement.

Although it occurs less commonly, you may also have applicants for positions who hold one of the following visas:

- F: students
- O: *individuals* with extraordinary abilities, demonstrated through sustained national or international acclaim in such areas as the sciences, education, business, athletics, arts, motion pictures, or television
- P: *groups* of artists, athletes, and entertainers who will receive temporary employment in the United States
- Q: exchange visitors in programs designated by U.S. Citizenship and Immigration Services
- R: religious workers who will be employed at least twenty hours per week by a nonprofit religious organization

It should not be assumed that people holding visas in these categories are automatically eligible for employment in the United States. For that reason, every job offer you make should be designated as contingent upon obtaining valid work authorization.

PUTTING IT ALL TOGETHER

Negotiating an offer and closing the deal is often a surprisingly complex process. Although there are frequently many more qualified candidates than there are faculty positions available, few candidates will accept an initial job offer as it is presented.

For this reason, the hiring authority should always approach the offer process with at least two plans in mind: Plan A (what is and is not negotiable for the preferred candidate) and Plan B (what you will do if the preferred candidate does not accept the offer even after negotiations?). Since, in the United States, hiring applicants who are neither citizens nor permanent residents often involves additional required steps before a candidate is eligible for legal employment, the candidate's legal authorization to work should be established as soon as possible during the offer process.

Despite your best efforts, some candidates will turn down an offer no matter how attractive you make it. They may have received an offer from another institution that's even more appealing than the best package you can assemble; they may prefer working in a different region for family, climate, or other reasons; or they may have had such a negative experience during the search process that they wouldn't accept an offer from your school on any terms.

Of these possibilities, it's only the last that you need be concerned about. If the problem stems from your search process, work immediately to fix it so that the issue doesn't arise with future candidates. If the candidate turns your offer down for any other reason, wish the person well and begin putting your backup plan in place, satisfied that you've at least done everything in your power to leave this candidate with a good impression of your program and school.

Chapter 6

Starting the New Faculty Member Off Right

There's an old saying in fund-raising that once the gift is received, your work has only just begun. A similar rule applies to faculty recruitment and hiring: Once an offer is accepted, your real work has only just begun. The process of recruiting and hiring a faculty member also includes making sure that the new person starts off right, is able to make an effective transition to your program, and is fully initiated into the culture of your institution.

In *The Essential Academic Dean or Provost*, I relate a story about an experience that's all too familiar to many faculty members who are new to an institution:

> There's an old joke about a college professor who dies and is standing before the Pearly Gates. St. Peter says, "Well, this has never happened before. In your lifetime, you did exactly as much good as evil. So, we'll give you a choice: Spend all day tomorrow in heaven, the next day in hell, and then tell me the day after that which one you prefer." The professor goes to heaven on the following day and finds that it's nice but rather boring. Everyone is dressed all in white. There's constant harp music. And there are no vices to provide a break in the routine. On the next day, the professor is greeted in hell with a huge reception. One of the devils says, "Oh, I read your book, and it was *fantastic, brilliant!*" Everyone treats the professor like a celebrity. Lunch is expertly catered, and the drinks are unlimited. When the two visits are over, St. Peter asks which place the professor prefers. "On the whole, I actually think I had a better time in hell." St. Peter thinks that an odd choice, but the decision has been made, and the professor is immediately sent to hell. All around there's nothing but fire and brimstone. People either ignore the professor entirely or utter rude remarks in passing. Finally, the professor finds the devil who had been so enthusiastic about the book and asks, "What's wrong? Everyone was so nice yesterday." The devil looks confused for a moment and then realizes what had happened. "Oh,

that?" he replies. "You see, yesterday we were interviewing you. Today you're faculty." (Buller 2015, 95–96)

That story strikes closer to home than we sometimes like to admit. For all the time and money we devote to the search process, we sometimes devote surprisingly little to making sure that the candidate we hire is successful.

From the faculty member's perspective, the power dynamic appears to have shifted once again. If the institution held all the power during the search process (because it had something the candidates wanted: a job) and the candidate held all the power during the negotiation process (because he or she had something the institution wanted: acceptance of the offer), that power has returned fully and irreversibly to the institution once the contract has been signed. It's no wonder that many newly hired faculty members feel that the university that had been so eager to court them suddenly seems to have become cold and indifferent now that they're "married."

To their credit, most institutions do try to help recently hired faculty members start their positions successfully through two overlapping, but somewhat different, processes: orientation and onboarding. Both of these words are travel metaphors and treat people's careers as though they were journeys.

The word *orientation* is derived from the Latin verb *orior*, which means "I rise up," and the word *orient* is derived from that verb's present participle: The orient is the land of the *rising* sun. So, on a journey, if you wanted to get your bearings, or your *orientation*, you could simply note where the sun rose each morning and know that that direction was east or the orient. If during that day's travels, you lost your sense of which way was east, you became *disoriented* and would need to be *reoriented* the next day.

The word *onboarding* is a nautical image. On cruises, the onboarding process involves learning what the emergency procedures are, what time meals are served, and where the various ports of call will be. Once the passengers have been successfully onboarded, it's possible for the ship to depart safely, with everyone knowing what they're supposed to be doing and (it's hoped) having a good time in the process.

In general, faculty orientation usually involves those processes necessary to make the person who has been hired as a full employee of the college or university: filling out forms, receiving keys, registering for benefits, learning basic policies and procedures, and becoming acquainted with fundamental administrative issues. Faculty onboarding usually involves those processes necessary to make the person who has been hired as a full member of the academic community. It tends to deal less with institutional policies and procedures than the orientation program does and focuses much more on what it means to be a college professor today.

If we compare these activities to how students are introduced to the institution, orientation is a bit like welcome week, while onboarding is a bit more similar to a first-year experience program. In fact, some schools even speak of a faculty first-year experience and extend the onboarding process over many months.

A common model for faculty onboarding is a monthly meeting with the provost, the dean, or another administrator in which those who have recently been hired talk about their experience, serve as a support group for one another, and participate in a workshop related to various aspects of faculty work. Common workshop topics include techniques for promoting active learning, teaching large classes effectively, strategies for identifying sources of external funding for research, grant writing, conducting productive meetings, and applying for promotion and tenure. The workshop series is often tied to a book about the faculty experience such as Robert Boice's *Advice for New Faculty Members* (2000), Jeff Buller and Bob Cipriano's *A Toolkit for College Professors* (2015a), Jeff Buller's *The Essential College Professor* (2010), Mary Clement's *First Time in the College Classroom* (2010), or Ken Bain's *What the Best College Teachers Do* (2004).

As you consider the best way to structure this type of experience for the type of institution you have and its philosophy of faculty development, consider the following thought experiment and how you might handle it.

THOUGHT EXPERIMENT 6.1: TROUBLING OBSERVATIONS

Imagine that you've been asked to participate in a faculty first-year experience program for those who have been hired at your institution. While some of the faculty members who participate in this program come from your own academic area, others are from different academic fields and known to you only as participants in this program. One faculty member from another department has given you cause to be concerned: Although this person was very upbeat and outgoing during the first few sessions, as the academic year wore on, you've noticed that he or she has become more and more withdrawn, barely saying anything during the meetings and avoiding eye contact with others in the room. What, if anything, should you do?

Faculty members who start their positions with a great burst of energy may gradually lose their enthusiasm and become more disengaged for any of a large number of reasons. In many cases, the excitement of having a new full-time job gradually becomes tempered by the realities of how challenging it can be to serve as a faculty member today. In other cases, problems in the workplace or at home can interfere with the person's commitment to work and cause him or her either to become or to seem to become less than fully engaged.

The situation described in the thought experiment appears to be more than just ordinary adjustment to the realities of being a college professor. Although you don't want to cross the boundaries of prying into matters that the faculty member considers personal, the situation described in the thought experiment probably calls for at least some degree of follow-up. In a way, it is probably a good thing that you're in a different discipline from that of the faculty member. He or she may feel freer talking to you about a problem than might be the case with someone in the same program or someone who might be involved in his or her evaluation. Particularly if there is a problem in the program itself, it can be easier for someone to share these concerns with an outsider than with someone he or she might associate with the problem's cause, not its solution.

Consider a brief visit to the faculty member's office during a time when he or she isn't meeting with students or colleagues. Mention the changes in behavior that you've observed without imputing blame or trying to psycho-analyze the person. You may be offering the help that's needed simply by being willing to listen. If the person does say that a problem has arisen that is affecting his or her attitude or performance, discuss the resources available that the person can turn to for help. If the person denies that a problem exists or is unwilling to confide in you, reiterate your willingness to talk again if that situation changes, but, for the moment, honor the faculty member's conclusion that your help is not needed. Under no circumstances should you report your concerns to the faculty member's supervisor since you have no way of knowing that person's role in the problem, if indeed a problem does exist.

ADDRESS THE ANXIETY OF TRANSITION

For some newly hired faculty members, the transition to your institution, while exciting, can also be a source of anxiety or loneliness. They may have moved to your area alone and know few other people in the community aside from those they met during their interviews, and, if they're members of an ethnic minority, they may experience the additional isolation of not having a local community of others who can understand their background and perspectives. If they moved with a family, there may be concerns about the ability of a spouse to find a job or of children to adapt to a new school.

Each new faculty member's challenges is likely to be different, and a series of regular check-ins that makes it clear that you're available if needed and that winds down over the course of a faculty member's first year can go a long way toward promoting an effective transition. Gentle reminders to the rest of the faculty about the challenges of adapting to a new environment might also encourage others to reach out and demonstrate a generous degree of hospitality and understanding. In truly difficult cases, your institution's employee assistance program may have additional resources that can help a new arrival overcome loneliness, isolation, or transition anxiety.

In order to make sure that the orientation and onboarding of new faculty members are more consistent across the institution, several schools have created in-house guidebooks that combine discussion of best practices throughout higher education with explanations of institutional policies and resources. An excellent example of such a resource is the guide *Giving and Getting Career Advice: A Guide for Junior and Senior Faculty*, which can be found as part of the ADVANCE Toolkit for Administrative Leaders at the University of Michigan at advance.umich.edu/resources/toolkit.pdf. This guide includes a valuable checklist of questions that new faculty members should be asking in order to increase their likelihood for succéss. Some of the questions suggested in this guide include, "What are appropriate ways to raise different kinds of concerns or issues and with whom?" "How do people find out about and get nominated for awards or prizes?" "What are the important committees to serve on?" and "How does one build a tenure file?" (Smock and Stephenson 2015, 11–12).

Developing a set of similar questions for new faculty members at your own college or university can serve to inform them of issues they may not have thought to ask about while underscoring that asking questions such as these is not only acceptable but even encouraged.

THOUGHT EXPERIMENT 6.2: THE NEW HIRE

Suppose that your department has been very stable and that you've finally been able to hire your first new faculty member in many years. The new assistant professor that you bring into your program is thus the youngest faculty member in the discipline by nearly two decades. In addition, your efforts to diversify your program have paid off: The new faculty member is from another country and comes from an ethnic minority that is severely underrepresented at your institution. You're confident that the person will be successful in all responsibilities associated with the job, but you're less certain about how comfortable he or she will be in your program's current social and cultural environment. What can you do to help your new faculty member adjust to his or her new situation?

In the situation described in this thought experiment, your best approach is probably to express to the faculty member your willingness to discuss any professional or personal challenges he or she may face in the new environment of your institution. Assuming that someone will feel alienated simply because he or she is different can be just as problematic as being insensitive to any challenges that may arise. Some people thrive in environments where everyone else is very different from them. Others feel lonely and anxious. So, you can't assume that a problem exists unless the person tells you so or you have other evidence indicating that your new faculty member is not adjusting well to the institution and its community.

If your new faculty member does indeed tell you that he or she feels isolated at your institution, consider all the resources he or she would have available in the area. Even if no other faculty members at the institution share the faculty member's ethnicity, there may be students of that ethnicity whom he or she can mentor, local cultural organizations whose outreach activities can provide assistance, or other faculty members who, although they have different backgrounds, are similarly feeling isolated and thus can help provide mutual support and assistance. Finding appropriate resources may require a good deal of creativity, but if you search broadly enough, you will almost always find an approach that can help a faculty member deal more effectively with the anxiety of transition.

PROVIDE THE TYPE OF START-UP HELP NEEDED

Although the majority of faculty members whose start-up package includes lab support will be well familiar with how to take advantage of the resources offered, there are occasionally faculty members who are setting up an independent laboratory for the first time. It's thus important that the resources an institution provides include not only space and equipment but also the guidance and human resources the person may need to make an effective start. Even when labs aren't involved, faculty members may need assistance setting up new computers in their offices, transitioning to a new e-mail or classroom management system, and discovering local procedures for getting items mailed, copies made, and expenses reimbursed.

One of the greatest sources of frustration for many new faculty members is to discover that the warm, supportive atmosphere they encountered during their interviews seems to have vanished almost immediately after they arrived to begin their jobs. While some new employees will need a great deal of assistance and others will require much less, it's important for them all to know that their success is important to the program and that people are available to help them make as smooth a transition as possible.

The assistance new faculty members need may be personal or social as much as it may be professional. Therefore, if you're in a position to do so, setting up a fund that senior faculty members can use to take junior faculty members out for lunch or coffee occasionally can help build collegiality throughout the program and provide new faculty members with the type of intangible support they may need.

BE REALISTIC ABOUT EXPECTATIONS

The notion that higher education fosters an environment of "publish or perish" has become so hackneyed that college professors sometimes roll their eyes when they hear others mention it. But the fact remains that at most institutions faculty members need to establish a solid record of refereed publications and/or external grants within a relatively short time frame. The standard sixth-year review for tenure arrives quickly enough, but most institutions now conduct a preliminary pre-tenure review in the faculty member's second or third year. If there isn't already sufficient evidence that the faculty member is on track for publications of sufficient quality and quantity by the time the tenure evaluation will occur, his or her contract can be nonrenewed with relatively little notice and very little opportunity for appeal.

While tenure-track faculty members receive their orientation, onboarding, or first-year faculty experience, it's important for these expectations to be laid out clearly and realistically. Certainly you want to convey the message that you have every confidence in the faculty member to achieve the ambitious goals you outline. But it's also a good practice to underscore how important the institution regards achievements in research and other scholarly activities and to indicate the consequences for not meeting the expectations you've set forth.

One useful tool in setting out these expectations is the development of a *faculty flight plan*: an outline of what a faculty member's goals should be, term by term, from hiring through evaluation for promotion and tenure. A well-constructed flight plan indicates not merely which courses the faculty member is expected to teach each term but also when various products of scholarship should be completed—and, even more importantly, when they should be *begun*, when they should be *halfway finished*, and when they should be *submitted for external review*.

Faculty flight plans can also help the faculty member understand how much committee work and other service can reasonably be expected at the same time that preparation of new courses and achievements in research are also under way. They can discourage faculty members from getting behind in their research because they volunteer to teach overloads, offer summer courses, or engage in other activities that provide quick income but detract from their long-range goals. Flight plans should be flexible instruments, developed in collaboration with the faculty member, that help the person achieve his or her individual goals at the same time that he or she is realistic about the institution's expectations. (For more on faculty flight plans, see Buller [2015, 367–370].)

WORK TO CHANGE INSTITUTIONAL POLICIES

Higher education has changed rapidly, but many institutional policies and criteria for evaluating faculty performance have failed to keep up with these changes. Some programs assume that every faculty member lives within a type of family structure that allows for uninterrupted focus on professional responsibilities. Many institutions also consider student ratings of instruction, committee involvement, external grants, and the number of refereed publications and their impact factors to be adequate evaluations of teaching, service, and research, respectively.

Even though these policies and criteria may have worked well in the past, they can actually be getting in the way of faculty success today. As a result, you can contribute to the long-term effectiveness of the faculty members you hire by being an advocate for some or all of the following policies if your institution doesn't already have them:

- family-friendly policies such as affordable on-campus childcare, tuition remission or discounts for dependents, and a tenure stop-clock policy that allows the tenure timetable to be interrupted when certain family issues (e.g., the birth of a child or the death of a close relative) arise
- holistic evaluation policies, which don't stop with measuring only those factors that are immediately measurable (e.g., the satisfaction scores that result from most student course evaluation processes) but also longitudinal impact (e.g., senior faculty member effectiveness in helping their junior colleagues advance in the profession and transition to new responsibilities and student success in subsequent courses, progress from pre-course or program to post-course or program, and acceptance rates into careers or graduate programs)
- instructional development policies, which reward people not just for how well their students learn but also for their contributions to teaching in areas such as service learning, the pioneering of new instructional methods, and mentoring students outside the classroom
- nontraditional scholarship policies, which recognize the importance of community-based action research, developing start-up companies or new products, promoting social entrepreneurship, performance and other

creative work, interdisciplinary research, and other activities that may be overlooked by narrower publication- and grant-oriented research policies
- nontraditional trajectory policies, which don't assume that everyone enters higher education by going directly from an undergraduate to a graduate degree and then moving systematically up the ladder from assistant to associate to full professor and which, instead, recognize that faculty members today increasingly move into and out of higher education to raise a family, take a job with a private industry, work on a political campaign, or engage in other activities that make them more valuable to us as well-rounded human beings

By making sure that our policies can accommodate these nontraditional trajectories, we increase the likelihood of success for a faculty that's diverse not just in terms of race and ethnicity but in career paths and goals as well.

THOUGHT EXPERIMENT 6.3: THE LOST OPPORTUNITY

Imagine that the academic year is coming to an end when one of your first-year faculty members comes to your office. You were very pleased that you were able to hire this candidate because he or she came to your program with superb credentials, an innovative approach to teaching, and an established record of research. In addition, the faculty member gave your program a much-needed increase in ethnic diversity. You are surprised (and very disappointed), therefore, when the faculty member announces that he or she has taken another job offer and won't be returning for a second year. When you ask why he or she wants to leave so soon, all you're given is a vague response about your program not being sufficiently "family friendly." The faculty member continues, "Other schools seem to have adapted better to the realities of today's faculty's need for work-life balance." Since the faculty member makes it clear that his or her mind is already made up with regard to leaving your school, what might you do so as not to lose the opportunity to retain such a valued employee next time?

You certainly don't have enough information from this thought experiment alone to recommend specific policy changes. At the very least, you'll want to explore further into why this person thought your institution was not supportive of families and how it could better adjust to what faculty members need in order to balance their personal and professional commitments.

In all likelihood, what you'll discover is that the faculty member had tried unsuccessfully to secure affordable daycare for children, home healthcare for elderly parents, or both. It may also be that your school's tenure and promotion timetable doesn't allow sufficient flexibility for scholars who are trying to balance personal commitments with professional responsibilities or who have had a nontraditional career path.

The bad news, of course, is that you've lost the opportunity to retain this valuable member of your staff. The good news is that you may be able to use this disappointment as leverage to promote some much-needed policy changes at your institution.

PROVIDE NEWLY HIRED FACULTY MEMBERS WITH MENTORS

One of the most effective practices in helping newly hired faculty members become successful is pairing them with more experienced faculty members as mentors. The best mentors are people who are not in a direct supervisory role over the faculty member (so assigning the chair or dean to be someone's mentor isn't a good idea) but who are familiar enough with the faculty member's specialty to provide practical advice.

When possible, mentors should come from different, although comparable, departments. When such an arrangement isn't possible, mentors should at least be people who, while they understand the faculty member's specialty, aren't directly in that specialty.

There may be times, for instance, when the problem a new faculty member wants to talk about involves his or her colleagues, and so some degree of distance is useful both to ensure a larger perspective and to alleviate any fears of reprisal. It's difficult to talk about the communication problems you're having with your research partner when the mentor you're sharing these concerns with is that research partner.

It's important to remember, too, that not every newly hired faculty member needs the same kind of mentor. Someone who's fresh out of graduate school may benefit from a mentor who can help smooth that person's way into the profession, while a more experienced faculty member who's merely new to your institution may benefit more from someone who can provide guidance about local traditions, who does what in various offices, and which policies may be different from those that the person knew elsewhere.

Failing to assign the right kind of mentor to the right person ends up being counterproductive. A more experienced faculty member will feel that the mentor is condescending if he or she assumes that the faculty member isn't familiar with the basics of the profession. A very inexperienced faculty member will feel betrayed if a mentor doesn't provide guidance about the politics found at the institution and how to establish one's own priorities for success.

PREPARE EXPERIENCED FACULTY MEMBERS TO BE COACHES AND MENTORS

Of course, if recently hired faculty members can benefit from being mentored by someone more experienced, we can't simply expect our senior faculty members to possess natural talent as a coach or mentor. Many people know how to succeed as a faculty member but can't articulate that knowledge for others, or they assume that the way in which they succeeded is the only possible route to faculty success.

Including training for coaches and mentors as part of your institution's professional development program is one of those initiatives that has no downside. More experienced faculty members become more engaged because they discover effective ways of passing on their insights on to new generations. Newly hired faculty members benefit because they're exposed to practical, one-on-one guidance right from the beginning of their careers.

There are a number of valuable resources to use in a training program for mentors. Lois Zachary's *The Mentor's Guide: Facilitating Effective Learning Relationships* (2012) and Julie Starr's *The Mentoring Manual: Your Step by Step Guide to Being a Better Mentor* (2014) both work well as a textbook for a workshop, module, or mini-course on faculty mentoring.

The University of New Mexico conducts an annual, multiday mentoring institute that combines plenary sessions, hands-on workshops, and other training opportunities that deal with effective mentoring (University of New Mexico 2016). ATLAS Leadership Training offers a half-day workshop on Best Practices in Coaching and Mentoring or a full-day workshop on Interpersonal Skills for Academic Leaders that are conducted on an institution's campus and include practical, experiential activities (ATLAS: Leadership Training for Higher Education 2015). Perrone-Ambrose Associates offers a combination of materials (including their *Mentoring in a Bag* set of books, assessments, and journals in a convenient tote), workshops, webinars, and other training opportunities (Perrone-Ambrose Associates, Inc. 2016).

Several other professional organizations offer training programs in mentoring for professionals in their disciplines. The type of training you choose will be a matter of your needs, budget, and time frame.

One useful tool you might consider making available is a mentor evaluation form. A form of this kind is helpful both for mentors and for the people they're mentoring. For the mentors, it provides feedback they can use to become more effective in the type of advice they're giving. For the people being mentored, it gives them a sense of control and engagement in a process where they might otherwise feel that they have very little voice and authority. A well-designed mentor evaluation form might look something like the following:

MENTOR EVALUATION FORM (SAMPLE)

Please rate me in each of the following areas on a scale of 1 (very poor) to 5 (very good).

As my mentor, you:

1) Encourage me to pursue assignments that capitalize on my strengths.
2) Give me visibility with higher levels of the administration.
3) Provide me with the freedom I need to do my job.
4) Set standards of excellence.
5) Make me acquainted with the institution's values and goals.
6) Hold me accountable.
7) Protect me from unnecessary stress.
8) Encourage me when I'm discouraged.
9) Give me guidance about institutional "politics."
10) Make performance expectations and priorities clear.
11) Take time to build trust.
12) Listen to my ideas even when you disagree.
13) Treat me with respect.
14) Serve as a good role model.
15) Won't let me give up.
16) Keep information confidential as appropriate.
17) Give me recognition when I deserve it.
18) Show a personal interest in me.
19) Support me when I take risks.
20) Help me understand the consequences of my decisions.
21) Are approachable and accessible.
22) Refrain from giving me inappropriate advice about my personal life.

STUDY WHAT GOES WRONG

Even though the ideal situation is for every search to end in the hiring of a faculty member who has a long and successful career at your institution, in reality, there will be disappointments and failures along the way. You can help improve the recruitment, hiring, and onboarding of faculty members if you track several different aspects of what went wrong in different searches, identifying patterns or trends so that you can continually improve the process. Among the various questions whose answers you may want to track include the following:

- Why don't people accept job offers? There will be times when the person we most want to hire for a position doesn't accept the offer we make. Knowing the reasons why can help us make better offers in the future. Some factors can't be controlled. The candidate may simply like a different part of the country or prefer working at a private institution when yours is public or vice versa. But other factors can suggest a strategy for improvement. If candidates repeatedly turn down your offer because the salary isn't sufficient, the facilities are aging, or the start-up package was too small, you'll have a strong case to make to the upper administration for making improvements in these areas. If candidates were alienated by what a particular faculty member said or the impression made by someone on the staff, you'll know where some better training may be required or at least who should take a less visible role in future searches.

- Why do people leave the institution willingly? When faculty members who are succeeding leave our institutions for other opportunities, a different sort of insight into how we can improve our processes for the future is gained. Once again, certain factors will be beyond your control: Someone may move to be closer to an aging parent or because another institution has offered the person a type of position that would be impossible at your school. But many people leave for issues of salary, working conditions, departmental politics, and other matters that can provide your institution with a wake-up call on the changes it needs to pursue in order to retain a larger number of successful faculty members in the future.

- Why do people leave the institution unwillingly? In chapter 2, we engaged in a thought experiment in which we recalled someone on the faculty who was fired, not renewed, or simply endured by everyone else in the program until he or she quit or retired. And then we explored the question, "What went wrong?" It's a useful practice to extend this activity from a thought experiment to an actual log of what goes wrong when people don't succeed in our environment. Have our search procedures not been stringent enough that people turn out not to have the capabilities they claimed during their interviews? Are we not looking carefully enough at each candidate's interpersonal skills and thus hiring people who have the right credentials but the wrong personalities for success? How can we fine-tune our recruitment and hiring process so as to reduce the number of unsuccessful faculty members we employ in the future?

PUTTING IT ALL TOGETHER

The process of recruiting, hiring, and onboarding faculty members is so well established at most institutions that many people may assume there's no other way to do it. But as we've seen throughout this book, there are many practices that can yield better results in everything from determining how an available position should be configured to bringing a recently hired faculty member fully into the community of academic citizens.

Recruiting and hiring faculty members is an expensive activity in every sense of the term. The one-time costs of advertising positions, conducting interviews, and providing start-up funds as well as the ongoing costs of salary, benefits, and research support can be substantial. The investment of time by members of the search committee, other members of the faculty and administration, and the applicants themselves is huge, and, if the wrong choice is made, all of that investment will have to be repeated in the near future.

In any enterprise as complex and expensive as a faculty hire, there are always ways to improve processes in order to increase the likelihood of achieving a good outcome (and often save money and time in the process). If you examine the search and hiring procedures in place at your institution and in your program, compare them to the best practices explored in this chapter, and note where improvements can be made, you'll have the basis for a practical blueprint for recruiting, selecting, and onboarding faculty members in the future.

Chapter 7

Drawing Conclusions

As we've seen throughout this book, hiring the right faculty member isn't the result of simply asking the right interview questions and trusting your instincts. It's the result of

- examining best practices in hiring at other colleges and universities, borrowing those practices that will work for your type of institution, and being innovative in developing new practices where no useful models exist.
- defining the position in such a way as to meet the needs of the discipline while still leaving the position broad enough to attract a diverse group of highly qualified applicants.
- asking the right questions during an interview and interpreting the answers we receive in a way that doesn't distract us from the most important issues.
- reviewing the impressions of everyone who met each candidate and using the collective wisdom to determine which applicant is most likely to succeed in the environment where he or she will be working.
- contacting your first choice quickly while having a clear understanding of the terms you're able to offer and the degree of flexibility you would have during negotiations with the candidate.
- giving the candidate a deadline by which he or she must accept the offer.
- developing an acceptable alternative plan if, for whatever reason, your first-choice candidate does not accept your offer.
- starting the new faculty member off right with a thorough, extended orientation that introduces the institution's policies, expectations, and resources in a manner that gives the person the best possible opportunity for success.
- providing the new faculty member with a properly prepared mentor.

In other words, hiring the right faculty member is a process that starts long before the actual search begins and continues long after the search ends. Colleges and universities never have all the resources they need. Since personnel are by far the largest component of any institution's budget (often accounting for 90% or more of annual expenditures), it's important for academic leaders to hire the right faculty member—every time. It can be tempting in the course of a busy term to delegate most of the responsibilities involved in defining the position, drafting the search advertisement, and selecting finalists to a search committee. Doing so is often a mistake. Hiring the right faculty member requires a holistic approach to thinking of your program as a system and then determining what that system needs in order to function most efficiently.

As faculty members, we train for many years to master the content and methods of our disciplines. But once we take on leadership roles, we discover that responsibilities like faculty search and recruitment can be just as complex as many of the scholarly activities we engage in as professors. It's my sincere hope that this short guide has helped you think about the faculty hiring process in new and more productive ways. If you have experiences that you'd like to share with me, I'd be happy to learn about them. You can reach me at jbuller@atlasleadership.com.

References and Resources

WORKS CITED

ATLAS: Leadership Training for Higher Education. 2015. "Who We Are." www
.atlasleadership.com/ATLAS_Leadership_Services/Welcome%21.html.

Bain, K. 2004. *What the Best College Teachers Do.* Cambridge, MA: Harvard University Press.

Boice, R. 2000. *Advice for New Faculty Members: Nihil Nimus.* Boston, MA: Allyn and Bacon.

Brafman, O., & Brafman, R. 2008. *Sway: The Irresistible Pull of Irrational Behavior.* New York: Doubleday.

Buller, J. L. 2010. *The Essential College Professor: A Practical Guide to an Academic Career.* San Francisco, CA: Jossey-Bass.

Buller, J. L. 2015. *The Essential Academic Dean or Provost: A Comprehensive Desk Reference.* 2nd ed. San Francisco, CA: Jossey-Bass.

Buller, J. L. 2017. *Best Practices for Faculty Search Committees: How to Review Applications and Interview Candidates.* San Francisco, CA: Jossey-Bass.

Buller, J. L., & Cipriano, R. E. 2015a. *A Toolkit for College Professors.* Lanham, MD: Rowman & Littlefield.

Buller, J. L., & Cipriano, R. E. 2015b. *A Toolkit for Department Chairs.* Lanham, MD: Rowman & Littlefield.

Cipriano, R. E. 2011. *Facilitating a Collegial Department in Higher Education: Strategies for Success.* San Francisco, CA: Jossey-Bass.

Clement, M. C. 2010. *First Time in the College Classroom: A Guide for Teaching Assistants, Instructors, and New Professors at All Colleges and Universities.* Lanham, MD: Rowman & Littlefield.

Fitzgerald, F. S. 1926. *All the Sad Young Men.* New York: Charles Scribner's Sons.

Hemingway, E. 1977. *The First Forty-Nine Stories.* Franklin Center, PA: Franklin Library.

Perrone-Ambrose Associates, Inc. 2016. "Mentoring and Coaching." www
.perrone-ambrose.com.

Smock, P. J., & Stephenson, R. 2015. *Giving and Getting Career Advice: A Guide for Junior and Senior Faculty*. Ann Arbor, MI: University of Michigan.

Starr, Julie. 2014. *The Mentoring Manual: Your Step by Step Guide to Being a Better Mentor*. New York: Pearson.

University of New Mexico. 2016. "UNM Mentoring Institute." mentor.unm.edu /conference.

Zachary, L. J. 2012. *The Mentor's Guide: Facilitating Effective Learning Relationships*. 2nd ed. San Francisco, CA: Jossey Bass.

MATERIALS FOR FURTHER STUDY

Buller, J. L. (May 2011). "The Need for Linking Innovation, Creativity, and Entrepreneurship." *Academic Leader 27*(5), 4–5.

Buller, J. L. (August 2011). "Strategic Hiring: Aligning Personnel Decisions with Long-Term Institutional Objectives." *Academic Leader 27*(8), 3, 8.

Buller, J. L. 2012. *The Essential Department Chair: A Comprehensive Desk Reference*. 2nd ed. San Francisco, CA: Jossey-Bass.

Buller, J. L. (March 2014). "What Every Search Committee Will Tell You." *Academic Leader 30*(3), 4–5.

Chun, E., & Evans, A. (Fall 2015). "Strategies for Enhancing Diversity in the Academic Department." *The Department Chair 26*(2), 20–21.

DeLuca, M. J., & DeLuca. N. F. (2010). *Best Answers to the 201 Most Frequently Asked Interview Questions*. New York: McGraw-Hill.

Hochel, S., & Wilson, C. E. (2007). *Hiring Right: Conducting Successful Searches in Higher Education*. San Francisco, CA: Jossey-Bass.

Reed, J. (2016). *101 Job Interview Questions You'll Never Fear Again*. East Rutherford, NJ: Penguin.

About the Author

Jeffrey L. Buller has served in administrative positions ranging from department chair to vice president for academic affairs at four very different institutions: Loras College, Georgia Southern University, Mary Baldwin College, and Florida Atlantic University. He is the author of thirteen books on higher education administration, a textbook for first-year college students, and a book of essays on the music dramas of Richard Wagner. Dr. Buller has also written numerous articles on Greek and Latin literature, nineteenth- and twentieth-century opera, and college administration. From 2003 to 2005, he served as the principal English-language lecturer at the International Wagner Festival in Bayreuth, Germany. More recently, he has been active as a consultant to the Ministry of Education in Saudi Arabia, where he is assisting with the creation of a kingdom-wide Academic Leadership Center. Along with Robert E. Cipriano, Dr. Buller is a senior partner in ATLAS: Academic Training, Leadership, & Assessment Services, through which he has presented numerous workshops on academic leadership, including sessions on how to recruit for, interview, and hire faculty members.

Other Books by Jeffrey L. Buller

Academic Leadership Day by Day: Small Steps That Lead to Great Success (2010)

Best Practices for Faculty Search Committees: How to Review Applications and Interview Candidates (2017)

Best Practices in Faculty Evaluation: A Practical Guide for Academic Leaders (2012)

Building Leadership Capacity: A Guide to Best Practices (with Walter H. Gmelch, (2015))

Change Leadership in Higher Education: A Practical Guide to Academic Transformation (2014)

The Essential Academic Dean or Provost: A Comprehensive Desk Reference, Second Edition (2015)

The Essential College Professor: A Practical Guide to an Academic Career (2009)

The Essential Department Chair: A Comprehensive Desk Reference, Second Edition (2012)

Going for the Gold: How to Become a World-Class Academic Fundraiser (with Dianne M. Reeves, (2016))

Positive Academic Leadership: How to Stop Putting Out Fires and Start Making a Difference (2013)

A Toolkit for College Professors (with Robert E. Cipriano, (2015))

A Toolkit for Department Chairs (with Robert E. Cipriano, (2015))

World-Class Fundraising Isn't a Solo Sport: The Team Approach to Academic Fundraising (with Dianne M. Reeves, (2016))

More about ATLAS

ATLAS: Academic Training, Leadership, & Assessment Services offers training programs, books, and materials dealing with collegiality and positive academic leadership. Its programs include the following:

- A Toolkit for College Professors
- A Toolkit for Department Chairs
- The Essential College Professor
- The Essential Department Chair
- The Essential Academic Dean or Provost
- Problem Solving for Academic Leaders
- Decision Making for Academic Leaders
- Best Practices in Faculty Evaluation
- Best Practices in Academic Fundraising
- Best Practices in Coaching and Mentoring
- Best Practices in Faculty Recruitment and Hiring
- Introduction to Academic Leadership
- Budgeting for Academic Leaders
- Teambuilding for Academic Leaders
- Creating a Culture of Student Success
- Change Leadership in Higher Education
- Time Management for Academic Leaders
- Interpersonal Skills for Academic Leaders
- Stress Management for Academic Leaders
- Organizational Culture in Higher Education
- Creating a Collegial Academic Environment
- Conflict Management for Academic Leaders
- Emotional Intelligence for Academic Leaders

- Effective Communication for Academic Leaders
- Positive Academic Leadership: A Systems Approach to Academic Leadership
- Authentic Academic Leadership: A Values-Based Approach to Academic Leadership
- Mindful Academic Leadership: A Mindfulness-Based Approach to Academic Leadership

ATLAS offers programs in half-day, full-day, and multiday formats. ATLAS also offers reduced prices on leadership books and materials that can be used to assess your institution or program:

- The Collegiality Assessment Matrix (CAM), which allows academic programs to evaluate the collegiality and civility of their faculty members in a consistent, objective, and reliable manner
- The Self-Assessment Matrix (S-AM), which is a self-evaluation version of the CAM
- The ATLAS Campus Climate and Moral Survey
- The ATLAS Faculty and Staff Engagement Survey

These assessment instruments are available in both electronic and paper formats. In addition, the free ATLAS E-Newsletter addresses a variety of issues related to academic leadership and is sent to subscribers.

For more information, contact:

ATLAS: Academic Training, Leadership, & Assessment Services
4521 PGA Boulevard, PMB 186
Palm Beach Gardens, FL 33418
800-355-6742; www.atlasleadership.com
E-mail: questions@atlasleadership.com